Healthful Living Cookbook
Caribbean Style

Carolle Hester Walker, BSc, MA

World rights reserved. This book or any portion thereof may not be copied or reproduced in any form or manner whatever, except as provided by law, without the written permission of the publisher, except by a reviewer who may quote brief passages in a review.

The author assumes full responsibility for the accuracy of all facts and quotations as cited in this book. The opinions expressed in this book are the author's personal views and interpretations, and do not necessarily reflect those of the publisher.

This book is provided with the understanding that the publisher is not engaged in giving spiritual, legal, medical, or other professional advice. If authoritative advice is needed, the reader should seek the counsel of a competent professional.

Copyright © 2015 TEACH Services, Inc.

Copyright © 2015 Carolle H. Walker

ISBN-13: 978-1-4796-0475-3 (Paperback)

ISBN-13: 978-1-4796-0476-0 (ePub)

ISBN-13: 978-1-4796-0477-7 (Mobi)

Library of Congress Control Number: 2015904689

Published by

www.TEACHServices.com • (800) 367-1844

"I wish above all things that thou mayest prosper and be in health, even as thy soul prospereth."
3 John 2

Testimonials

"Carolle Walker has been preparing vegetarian dishes for a long time, and over the years she has perfected her skills, producing several very tasty recipes for her family, friends, work, and church gatherings. I have enjoyed many of her creations including patties and steaks made with meat substitutes and vegetable casseroles and grain-based salads. Her recipes are well worth sharing." *Carol Leacock, RD*

"I used to think that growing up on Caribbean food meant that I could never find that special flavor without having some kind of meat on my plate. But every time I try one of her inspired vegan dishes I become more and more convinced that being vegan is possible without sacrificing that Caribbean flavor. I am talking about the vegan/vegetarian cuisine of Carolle Walker, my mother.

"She also takes many other styles of foods that I love so much and adds her own flare. Whether its her signature vegan/vegetarian meat patties, vegan/vegetarian meatballs, or frozen papaya dessert, I get introduced to a new look of an old favorite almost every time I'm in her kitchen. Her super cream of pumpkin soup is especially delectable.

"The best part about each dish she creates is that you're guaranteed that it is not just good to taste, but good for your body. As a nutritionist and nutrition educator, you can almost taste the science of nutrition blended with the art of cooking in every bite! Be sure to buy a copy of this cookbook; you'll like it." *Gene-Anthony A. Hay, son*

"After trying Carolle Walker's pumpkin soup, I realized what a talent she has for cooking. Great taste, great job! I am sure this soup will be a tremendous success!" *Vere Weaver*

"Along with its various health benefits, I definitely noticed a huge improvement in my skin when I maintained a vegan diet. My acne flare-ups were dramatically reduced, which has further convinced me that a vegan diet is the most beneficial to our health all around." *Nadia-Lynn A. Hay, daughter*

"Carolle Walker's recipes are mouth-wateringly delicious. Nutritious and easy to prepare, they make both a vegan's or vegetarian's life simple, healthy, and good. Success!" *Glenda-mae Greene, PhD*

"I have truly enjoyed some of Ms. Walker's extraordinary collection of rich, flavorful vegan recipes. Most of them were created by her and were delightfully made to tempt any palate. I also had the opportunity to sit in on one of her cooking classes at the church in Northeast Palm Bay, Florida. This session was very informative. We prepared a couple of vegan dishes from scratch, and I first sampled cashew cheese, which had a really nice taste and consistency to say the least. At the end of that session, Ms. Walker gave me an array of complementary vegan recipes for me to try at home, and I've been hooked ever since." *Dave Urquhart*

"In today's world most of the chronic diseases we know are largely a result of substandard food ingredients and nutritional deficiencies, not to mention the lack of routine physical exercise. After attending a few of Ms. Walker's nutrition classes and trying her homemade vegan recipes, I've been able to incorporate this healthier style of vegan food preparation into my daily routine. I have also noticed that I'm more energetic, and as a person with diabetes and high blood pressure, I am able to eat a greater variety of foods and delicious, nutritious meals while at the same time better control my diabetes and high blood pressure. Ya mon! Try it nuh!" *Ira Urquhart*

"I have known Carolle Walker for twelve years, and she has always been careful about what she eats. Carolle has encouraged people to adopt and maintain a healthy lifestyle. I have attended many of her cooking classes and tried some of her recipes, and I have found them to be very tasty and nutritious. I highly recommend this cookbook to others and hope you will try these delicious recipes too." *Mavis West, RN*

Dedication

I dedicate this book to my children,

Gene-Anthony A. Hay

and

Nadia-Lynn A. Hay,

and my friends and all those who have chosen to

modify their behavior by eating healthier and engaging in

a more active lifestyle so as to

improve their health for the rest of their lives.

Acknowledgement

I am extremely grateful to God for giving me an opportunity to learn from His Word about the first and best diet that He instituted for mankind, to keep us healthy and strong (Genesis 1:29). He made humanity and knew exactly what we would need to keep our bodies functioning properly. He also gave us the ability to use the food He provides to make delicious and nutritious dishes.

I want to thank my many friends, coworkers, and even some of my clients who have encouraged me to write this cookbook. Thanks to my children Gene-Anthony Hay and Nadia-Lynn Hay for being the taste testers of my vegan dishes. I especially thank Nadia-Lynn for doing all the typing and corresponding with the publisher and sending the manuscript to them.

In addition, I want to thank my children and my friends Carol Leacock, RD; Dr. Glenda-Mae Green; Dave Urquhart; Ira Urquhart; Vere Weaver; Judith Weaver, RN; and Mavis West, RN, for your encouraging testimonials and interesting recipes. To David Alleyne, you might not know this, but you inspired me to create "soy curl fritters." When I invited you and your wife, Dorett, to my birthday celebration in November 2012, you answered with this question, "Will you have cod fish cakes?" Since I am a vegan, my reply was, "No, but you should come." Then the thought came immediately, "Use the soy curls to make some fritters as a substitute, and get them to taste like codfish cakes." I tried one, and it was delicious! Thus, a recipe was born thanks to your question!

A very special thank you to Dr. Glenda-Mae Greene, herself an author, and her mom, Carol Greene. They both continue to encourage and guide me with this project, and I greatly appreciate that.

All who have tasted my vegan dishes firmly believe I should give others the opportunity to buy this book so that they too can use these recipes to prepare meals that will help in improving their nutrition status.

Preface

The *Healthful Living Cookbook: Caribbean Style* has been in the works for a long time. However, I do believe that this is the appropriate time for such a publication. The recipes in this book are in accordance with the first diet given by the best and first dietitian—God. He told us about all the foods we need to eat in Genesis 1:29, which describes a plant-based diet. It states, "Behold, I have given you every herb bearing seed, which is upon the face of all the earth, and every tree, in the which is the fruit of a tree yielding seed; to you it shall be for meat."

I hope that the book will answer many questions related to healthier living and dispel many fears and doubts by those who honestly want to get away from eating animal products but don't know where to start. In recent years there has been a growing trend to switch to a vegetarian lifestyle, and many start with giving up meat in hopes of ultimately giving up all animal products and becoming vegans. However, for many people the real problem is a fear of making a change.

Many people believe that a vegan/vegetarian diet will fail to supply their body with important nutrients. Others fear that the food will not taste good, that it will cost too much to switch to a plant-based diet, or that it will take too much time to prepare. On the contrary, a plant-based diet results in dishes that are lower in fat, sodium, and cholesterol and higher in fiber and other nutrients. These benefits help prevent and/or control many diseases such as obesity, heart disease, diabetes, hypertension, high cholesterol, cancer, and others. This book aims to alleviate your fears and doubts by providing mouth-watering recipes that are easy to prepare. God, our Creator, loves us so much and knows exactly what our bodies need to function. We do not need to be afraid that a plant-based diet will not supply the needed nutrients, for God made us and the plants that He instructed us to eat.

As a vegan with many years of nutrition and health experience, I am confident that the recipes and meals in this book are nutritious, appetizing, and packed with essential and non-essential nutrients, which is now being backed up by scientific studies by such groups as the American Dietetic Association.

I hope that this cookbook will encourage you to make healthy choices because your body is the temple of God. Blessings.

Carolle

Table of Contents

Introduction	15
Nutrition Corner	17
Keeping Fit: The Importance of Exercise	19
Healthy Choices	20
Health Myths	21
Appetizers/Hors D'oeuvres	23
Entrées	33
Side Dishes	61
Soups	69
Salads and Vegetable Dishes	73
Soup Bases and Sauces	77
Bread, Biscuits	87
Desserts	89
Beverages	99
Miscellaneous	103
Sample Menu	104
Weights and Measurements	105
Resources and Reference Materials	106
Glossary	107
Index	113
About the Author	117

Introduction

The main objective for writing this book is to encourage, inspire, educate, and assist others in making changes to their diet so as to take a step towards healthier living.

Cooking, nutrition and education activities have been a part of my life for many decades. Especially coming from the tropical island of Jamaica with a culture that envelopes many different cultures, such that it has the appropriate national motto, "Out of Many, One People," there is a little of each culture and ethnicity in each one of us. This makes for diversity and variety in the meals we prepare. In light of this, my recipes are created to highlight a taste of Caribbean cuisine among other cuisines. Growing our own foods, fruits, vegetables, and herbs is a part of the Caribbean lifestyle, as is eating the fresh, naturally grown foods we cultivate.

As mentioned in the preface, there has been in the past twenty-five to thirty years an influx of great revolution as far as health consciousness is concerned, with an emphasis on healthy eating and exercise. Many people are going from a diet of animal products to being vegetarians. But who is a vegetarian? There are three categories: 1) lacto-vegetarians, use dairy; 2) lacto-ovo vegetarians, use dairy and eggs; and 3) vegans, use no animal products, dairy, or eggs. The vegan diet is the best diet since it was given by God in the Garden of Eden. He told us what to eat in Genesis: fruits, nuts, grains, seeds, and vegetables. God made us and the food we eat. He knows that they supply all the essential and non-essential nutrients that the scientists say we need to promote growth and keep our bodies healthy.

The change from a diet of animal products to veganism is a holistic project that is geared to positively affect the body, mind, and spirit. It should be made in a sensible, gradual, and well-calculated manner. Your doctor should play a part by doing blood tests to ensure that blood fractions are at appropriate levels. Then you can gradually delete animal products from your diet daily and simultaneously include the fruits, vegetables, nuts, seeds, legumes, and grains. Ensure adequate water per day. Remember to get your exercise, fresh air, and sunshine, which is a powerful source of vitamin D.

I believe that my life experiences have given me the ability to create recipes that are nutritionally well-balanced, delicious, attractive, and include all the food groups and essential and non-essential nutrients in accordance with the Recommended Daily Allowances (RDAs, see glossary) for Americans. The recipes are naturally high in fiber and low in saturated fats, sodium, and sugar. The sugars I use in my recipes are: Sugar In The Raw® or organic sugar from sugarcane. I do not use honey in my recipes since this is an animal product. No artificial sweeteners are used because they have side effects. You can actually make your own cane sugar by following a simple method (see the recipe toward the end of the book).

From my observation and from talking to many people over the years, I have learned that many have a problem knowing how to prepare delicious vegan entrées. Because of this, the

Healthful Living Cookbook

largest category of recipes in the book is "entrées" to allow for a great variety and prevent boredom. These recipes are also fairly easy to follow and prepare. Some will take longer to make than others, but larger amounts can be prepared and some frozen for later use. The ingredients for these recipes can be purchased at most supermarkets or health food stores, and some ingredients can be made from scratch as instructed.

Some of the other reasons people are becoming vegans or vegetarians are that (1) animals are being fed foods containing substances that are unhealthy for both animals and humans and (2) some plants are being grown with artificial fertilizers and sprayed with pesticides. Another reason is that genetically modified organisms (GMOs; see glossary) have tainted both conventionally produced, as well as some organic foods. The wisest way to avoid using the above tainted foods is to use organic foods or naturally grown foods. Look for products with the "USDA Organic" seal and the "Non-GMO Project-Verified" seal (see glossary). The seals indicate to consumers that foods are being checked to ensure the avoidance of GMOs during production. It is also a good idea to try growing your own food as much as possible using natural fertilizers such as humus (see glossary).

I am grateful to have had the opportunity to create these recipes and write this book for you, having prepared the dishes for many family members, friends, and myself. I appreciate my daughter and my friends who have shared some of their original recipes with me, which are included in these pages. It is my hope that you will benefit from and delight in cooking the recipes in this book!

On the next few pages, before the recipe section, there are some general nutrition principles and cooking tips that I hope will provide you with more knowledge about your health. Blessings.

Nutrition Corner

Nutrition is a preventive science that deals with the process by which all living organisms take in, assimilate, and utilize food for energy, growth, repair of worn-out tissues, and all other body functions. In this section we will also discuss good nutrition versus malnutrition.

In order to maintain good nutrition, the dietary guidelines developed by the United States Department of Agriculture (USDA) recommend a diet that (1) includes a variety of foods each day that supply the essential and non-essential nutrients, which are proteins (about 50 grams per day), carbohydrates, fats, vitamins, and minerals; (2) is low in fat—saturated fat and cholesterol; (3) provides adequate starch and fiber (20–35 grams of fiber per day) according to the National Cancer Institute; (4) is low in sugar and sodium.

The Recommended Daily Allowances (RDAs, see glossary) is the suggested daily amount of different nutrients necessary for good nutrition. The Food Guide Pyramid is a model developed by the USDA as a graphic illustration to make it easy to understand the RDAs and dietary guidelines, which tells you how much you should eat from each food group. The main food groups are (1) grains; (2) fruits and vegetables; (3) meats, which includes beans and nuts; and (4) fats, oils, and sugars.

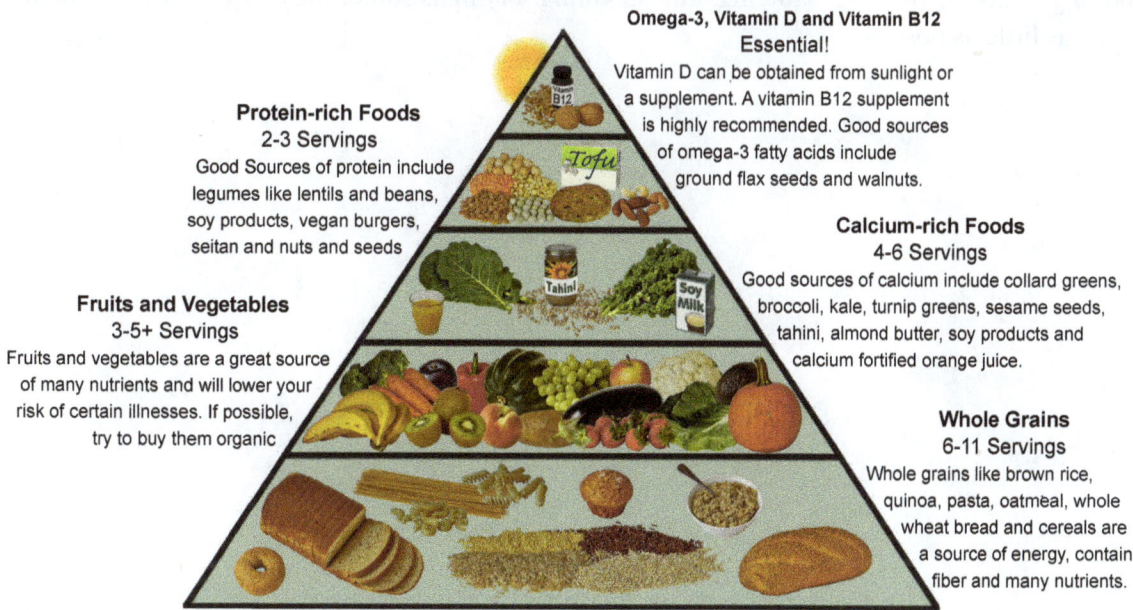

Copyright © 2011 by Wanda Embar, Vegan Peace: http://www.veganpeace.com.

When diet is lacking one or more essential or non-essential nutrients for a period of time, this leads to malnutrition. A constant imbalance in the daily diet can result in diseases like obesity, heart disease, high blood pressure, stroke, diabetes, cancer, and even dental and digestive problems.

Along with all of the recommended foods and nutrients, drinking enough water is essential and extremely important since it is the most abundant non-nutritious food component in our body. Water makes up approximately 70 percent of your body weight. The ideal amount of water intake is approximately half your body weight in ounces. Whether you are a vegan, vegetarian, or one who uses animal products, the dietary guidelines and RDAs are the same. Vegans and vegetarians get their nutrients from plant-based foods—fruits, vegetables, nuts, grains, and seeds. Lacto-ovo vegetarians sometimes use milk and eggs, while vegans use no animal products. According to the American Dietetic Association (now the Academy of Nutrition and Dietetics), "Plant sources of protein alone can provide adequate amounts of essential and non-essential amino acids" (Journal of the American Dietetic Association 96, no. 3 [March 1996], pp. 230, 231).

The National Center for Nutrition and Dietetics went so far as to write an article titled "Feeding Your Baby the Vegetarian Way" in which they pointed out that a vegetarian diet can provide adequate nutrition for children as long as the meals are appropriately planned. Breastfed babies of vegetarians may need vitamin B12 supplement as well as vitamin D, if there is limited exposure to sunlight. Babies on a vegan diet and weaned from breastfeeding should be fed a soy-based formula, not soymilk, as this milk does not have all the appropriate mix of nutrients needed by infants less than one year old.

Proper nutrition involves a well-rounded, adequate diet along with sunshine, fresh air, and regular exercise. Proper nutrition also involves appropriate cooking methods such as baking, boiling, braising, broiling, sautéing, and steaming. Frying is sometimes necessary but should be used as little as possible.

Keeping Fit: The Importance of Exercise

One definition of exercise suggests that it is activity to develop and strengthen the body. This is a simple definition that explains the word perfectly. Exercise is extremely important for good circulation. Coupled with good nutrition, exercising thirty minutes per day for five to six days per week can make a world of difference in your overall health.

Some benefits of exercise include:

1. Having a heart and lungs that function in a healthy manner to improve the body's ability to resist diseases and maintain a good immune system.

2. Improving the body's supply of energy to meet the demands placed on it by work and the other activities of daily living.

3. Maintenance of adequate weight for your height, frame, age, and activity level.

4. Having a good, positive feeling and self-worth, which helps to improve your mental, emotional, social, and spiritual well being.

5. Helping to control the body's ability to metabolize carbohydrates and to positively manage diabetes.

6. Maintaining adequate weight, which helps control high blood pressure and high cholesterol in the blood and decreases the risk of heart attacks.

It must be remembered that exercise, despite its importance, must go hand in hand with good nutrition. So what constitutes exercise? Any activity that helps you move your limbs and joints counts. Walking is great form of exercise. Again, this could be daily or at least five to six days per week. Some other simple activities to do include gardening, housework, riding a bicycle, lifting weights, or bending and stretching. Assisted range of motion is needed by those who can't walk or help themselves.

Let each of us exercise and properly take care of our bodies since they are the temple of God: "Know ye not that ye are the temple of God, and that the spirit of God dwelleth in you?" (1 Corinthians 3:16).

Get moving and live better!

Healthy Choices

Egg Substitutes

- Use 3 tablespoons ground flaxseed, plus 1/8 teaspoon baking powder, plus 3 tablespoons water in place of 1 egg. This especially works well for baking quick breads.

- Use ½ a ripe banana, mashed, plus ¼ teaspoon baking powder in place of 1 egg. A ½ cup applesauce may also be used instead of a banana. This especially works well for baking quick breads.

- Sauté ¼ cup of firm tofu, scramble and season to taste, in place of 1 egg. Use curry powder, turmeric, or saffron for coloring.

Organic vs. Non-organic
As much as possible, buy only "Non-GMO Project Verified" and "USDA organic" products. Read the labels carefully! It is important to cook with quality ingredients.

Water, Water, Water
An important factor in maintaining good health is drinking enough water. Each day you should drink ½ of your body weight in ounces.

Health Myths

Statement:
Diabetes is caused by eating too much sugar.

Answer:
False. Diabetes is a condition in which there is an inadequate production of insulin by the pancreas or an adequate production of insulin but the inability of the body to properly use the insulin. Both of the above situations lead to faulty metabolism of carbohydrates. Because of this, diabetics must be careful to control the intake of carbohydrates, which includes sugar. Exercise to avoid obesity and be aware of your family history.

Statement:
High blood pressure (hypertension) is a result of eating too much salt.

Answer:
False. High blood pressure is an elevation of blood pressure above the normal range, which increases the risk of cardiovascular disease, also known as heart disease. When there is high blood pressure, care must be taken to decrease the intake of salt, which is sodium chloride. It is the sodium that increases the risk of hypertension, so it is important to watch for foods that are high in sodium in any form. High body weight and family history of high blood pressure are high risk factors.

Ask your doctor about your blood pressure and testing for diabetes.

Appetizers/Hors D'oeuvres

Carolle's Cream of Pumpkin Soup

4 cups diced pumpkin, peeled
1 cup chopped onion
1 cup chopped celery
½ cup chopped green onions
1 cup diced carrots

½ cup canola/olive oil
1 teaspoon pepper sauce
1 tablespoon Bragg Liquid Aminos
1–2 cups coconut milk
4 cups vegetable stock

Directions

- In a large skillet, sauté diced pumpkin and all vegetables in oil for 5 minutes
- Add stock, Bragg Liquid Aminos, and pepper sauce and continue to cook another 10 minutes
- Pour in blender and purée until smooth
- Add coconut milk and return to fire
- Simmer for 5 additional minutes
- Serve in small bowls with small dumpling twists

Stock

1 cup chopped celery
2 cups chopped carrots
1 cup chopped onions
¼ cup canola oil

1 tablespoon thyme leaves
1 tablespoon chopped basil
6 cups water

- Put all ingredients in large stockpot and boil for 15–20 minutes.

Little Dumpling Twists

1 cup whole wheat flour or rice flour
¼ cup water

- Mix flour and water until it forms a dough
- Cut into small pieces and roll out, then twist and cook in the soup

Banana Fritters

2 fingers of ripe bananas
1 cup whole wheat, rice, or soy flour
1 tablespoon cinnamon
1 tablespoon nutmeg
½ tablespoon ground vanilla beans

1 teaspoon sea salt
¼ cup pecan meal (optional if allergic)
¼ cup almond or rice milk
¼ cup canola oil

Directions

- Crush bananas in mixing bowl
- Add all dry ingredients to the bananas and mix together
- Add milk and mix everything into a batter
- Spoon onto oiled baking sheet (1 tablespoon each) and bake at 400 degrees F until golden brown
- Serve with your favorite fruit sauce

Appetizers/Hors D'oeuvres

Nuts, Nuts, Nuts

1 cup cashews

1 cup peanuts

1 cup slivered or whole almonds

1 cup chopped Brazil nuts

Directions

- Put each type of nut in a special bowl; do not mix nuts
- Place small scoops in each cup and allow guests to serve themselves

Pumpkin Bites

2 cups cubed pumpkin
1 tablespoon cinnamon (optional)
½ cup coconut sauce (see recipe on page 81)

Directions

- Peel, slice, and cook the pumpkin; then cut into cubes to make 2 cups
- Arrange on a serving dish
- Sprinkle with onion powder (optional)
- Put a toothpick in each cube
- Pour coconut sauce over pumpkin bites and serve

Appetizers/Hors D'oeuvres

Soy Curl Fritters

4 ounces Butler Soy Curls™
½ cup whole wheat or rice flour
½ cup chopped green and red peppers
½ cup finely chopped tomatoes
1 tablespoon onion powder
1 teaspoon garlic salt

1 tablespoon veggie soup base seasoning (see recipe on page 77)
1 tablespoon dried parsley
1 tablespoon hot sauce
1 cup warm water
½ cup canola oil

Directions

- Soak Butler Soy Curls™ in warm water for 5 minutes
- Mix all ingredients, except oil, in mixing bowl; you may need more flour
- Heat oil in large skillet
- Spoon 2 tablespoons of the mixture into the heated oil and brown on both sides
- Take out of skillet and drain on wax paper
- Repeat until the batter is gone
- Serve as an appetizer, snack, or on a bun with tomato slices

Hors D'oeuvre Meatballs

1 chopped onion
½ cup gluten mince (see recipe on page 34)
½ cup crushed tofu
½ cup ground pecans
1 chopped garlic clove
½ cup wheat germ
½ cup whole wheat bread or flaxmeal crumbs
¼ cup cornstarch
1 tablespoon chopped parsley
¼ teaspoon oregano (optional)
1 teaspoon Bragg Liquid Aminos
½ cup water or as needed
2 cups tomato sauce
½ cup canola oil

Directions
- Blend onion, tofu, and gluten mince
- Combine all ingredients in mixing bowl and form into a stiff mixture
- Form into mini vegan meatballs and brown in hot oil in skillet
- Remove and drain on wax paper
- Put in baking dish
- Cover with tomato sauce and bake at 350 degrees F for 30 minutes
- Insert toothpicks into each meatball and serve

Vegetable Carrousel and Dip

1 cup baby carrots
1 cup cherry tomatoes
1 cup cauliflower spears
1 cup broccoli spears
1 cup cucumber logs
½ cup fresh parsley (garnish)
1 cup homemade hummus
  or other dips of choice

Directions
- Wash all vegetables and tomatoes
- Wash and chop fresh parsley
- Arrange the veggies and tomatoes on a chip-and-dip set, divided salad dish, or platter
- Sprinkle with parsley
- Put dip in bowl and set in the center of the vegetable carrousel

Appetizers/Hors D'oeuvres

Vere's Pumpkin Fritters

2 cups boiled, crushed pumpkin
1 cup whole wheat or rice flour
½ cup almond meal
2 teaspoons grated nutmeg
1 teaspoon cinnamon
1 tablespoon vanilla (alcohol free)
  or ½ tablespoon ground vanilla beans
1 tablespoon pear essence (alcohol free)
1 tablespoon brown sugar or molasses
½ teaspoon sea salt (optional)
½–¾ cup coconut milk
½ cup canola oil

Directions

- Mix all ingredients together into a thick batter
- Spoon into hot oil in a skillet and fry until golden brown on both sides or spoon onto oiled baking sheet and bake at 400 degrees F until done and golden brown
- May serve with sauce

Homemade Salsa

2 large finely cubed tomatoes
1 chopped onion
1 tablespoon freshly chopped parsley
1 medium chopped cucumber

1 small finely chopped garlic clove
1 tablespoon lemon juice
2 teaspoons hot pepper sauce (optional)

Directions
- Mix all ingredients together
- Chill in the refrigerator before serving

Entrées

Gluten Roast

4 cups gluten flour (Bob's Red Mill)
2 cups whole wheat flour
½ cup nutritional yeast flakes
2 tablespoons homemade veggie soup base seasoning

2 tablespoons onion powder
2 tablespoons garlic powder
1 teaspoon Bragg Liquid Aminos
4 cups warm water

Directions

- Mix all dry ingredients together
- Add warm water and mix well with spoon or your hands (use gloves)
- Knead slightly into one large ball
- Divide dough into 4 and make 4 logs
- Place logs in boiling broth, and cook on medium heat for 1–1 ½ hours
- When done, remove from pot, cool, and slice (1/8–1/4-inch thick)
- Serve with homemade Bar-B-Q sauce (see recipe on page 80) or another favorite sauce; serve with vegetables, rice or potatoes, or on a sandwich; or place the whole roast in a roast pan with mini potatoes, whole small onions, small carrots and green beans. Pour on Bar-B-Q sauce mix to cover roast and vegetables. Then cover pan and cook at 375 degrees F for 30–35 minutes. Remove roast, slice, and serve with favorite side dish.

Broth for cooking gluten logs

10–12 cups water for stock
½ cup Bragg Liquid Aminos (or soy sauce)
3 tablespoons homemade veggie soup base seasoning
2 cups tomato sauce (or traditional canned pasta sauce)

Suggestion

Make a large batch to be used for several meals. Chop some, cube some, slice some, and freeze it in freezer bags to save time for later.

Healthful Living Cookbook

Gluten Mince

- Make gluten roast dough (recipe on page 33) and broth (use less tomato sauce)
- Cut dough in much smaller pieces and cook in broth for 1 hour
- Remove from broth and cool in freezer or refrigerator for 20–30 minutes
- Remove from refrigerator/freezer and chop in blender
- Cool in refrigerator and pack in several freezer bags for later use in vegan mince loaf, vegan patties, spaghetti sauce, or other recipes
- Label and date freezer bags before freezing

Braised Gluten Roast Strips

2 cups gluten roast strips
  (cut gluten roast into strips)
1 cup chopped red and green peppers
1 cup chopped onions
1 cubed/chopped tomato
1 tablespoon onion powder
1 crushed and chopped garlic clove

1 tablespoon fresh chopped basil
2 teaspoons hot pepper sauce
2 teaspoons browning
1 teaspoon Bragg Liquid Aminos
¼ cup canola oil
½ cup water

Directions

- Sauté all vegetables and seasonings in large skillet
- Add gluten roast strips and mix with vegetables
- Continue to braise strips and vegetables for 5 minutes
- Serve with seasoned brown rice, rice and peas, seasoned bulgur wheat, or another favorite side dish and salad

Entrées

Gluten Chick Patties

3 cups gluten flour
1 cup whole wheat or brown rice flour
¾ cup pecan meal (optional)
¼ cup nutritional yeast flakes
¼ cup veggie soup base seasoning (see recipe on page 77)
2 tablespoons onion powder
2 teaspoons garlic powder
2 teaspoons Bragg Liquid Aminos or sea salt (optional)
3 cups warm water

Directions

- Mix all dry ingredients together
- Add warm water; mix gently but quickly with hands (use gloves)
- Form into large dough log
- Divide in half and make 2 logs
- Cut first log into ½-inch thick pieces and make patties
- Use second log to make gluten chick bits for other recipes, such as Gluten Chick Salad
- Put patties and bits in broth and boil for 30–40 minutes

Broth for cooking patties

12 cups water
¼ cup veggie soup base seasoning
2 teaspoons onion powder

Directions

- Bring to a boil in large pot; decrease heat and simmer for 15 minutes

35

Curried Gluten Bits

2 cups homemade gluten chick bits (see gluten chick patties recipe)
1 chopped onion
1 diced tomato
1 cup green and red sweet peppers
1 pressed and chopped garlic clove
2 sprigs of fresh or dried thyme
1 tablespoons hot pepper sauce
2 tablespoons curry powder
1 teaspoon Bragg Liquid Aminos
¼ cup canola oil

Directions
- Sauté vegetables and seasonings
- Add curry powder, pepper sauce, and Bragg Liquid Aminos to sautéed mix and continue cooking for 1 minute longer
- Add gluten bits and mix
- Cover and allow to simmer for 15–20 minutes
- Serve with a favorite side dish

Entrées

Hot or Cold Gluten Chick Salad

2 cups homemade gluten chick bits (see gluten chick patties recipe)

¾ cups homemade vegan mayo (see recipe on page 78)

1 cup chopped celery

1 cup homemade celery soup

½ cup chopped onion

½ cup chopped green and red sweet peppers

½ cup finely diced or shredded carrots

½ cup finely chopped almonds (or your favorite nut)

1 cup cooked brown rice

Toppings
1 cup bread crumbs
1 cup finely chopped walnuts (optional)
2 tablespoons light margarine

- Melt margarine, then add walnuts and breadcrumbs. Mix well.

Directions

- Make celery soup; make like cream of pumpkin soup on page 28
- Cook rice with sea salt (if needed)
- Mix all ingredients for salad together and eat cold, or pour the mixture into an oiled baking dish and sprinkle the topping evenly over it and bake at 350 degrees F until golden brown, approximately 25 minutes

Stir-Fry Vegetables with Gluten Roast Strips/Bits

2–3 cups gluten roast strips or gluten chick bits
2 cups green and red sweet pepper strips
2 medium tomatoes, cut into bite-size pieces
1 large onion, sliced in strips
1 cup shredded green cabbage
1 cup shredded carrots
2 cups broccoli spears
1 cup whole frozen green beans
2 tablespoons chopped fresh basil
1 tablespoon green thyme leaves
1 tablespoon Bragg Liquid Aminos
1 tablespoon browning
½ cup olive or canola oil
2 teaspoons hot pepper sauce (optional)

Directions

- Wash and prepare all vegetables
- In large skillet heat oil on medium high heat and add all vegetables, except carrots; stir well
- Remove vegetables from skillet and set aside
- Put gluten strips/bits in skillet and stir-fry for 3 minutes
- Return vegetables to the skillet and mix with gluten strips; add carrots, seasonings, and browning, and continue to stir-fry for 5 more minutes
- Serve with your favorite side dish

Curried Seasoned Soy Curls

4 ounces of Butler Soy Curls™
2–3 cups water
1 cup chopped onion
1 clove chopped garlic
½ cup chopped tomato
1 cup chopped sweet peppers (red and/or green)
1 tablespoon chopped parsley
1 tablespoon chopped rosemary
2 tablespoons curry powder
1 tablespoon hot pepper sauce (optional)
2 teaspoons Bragg Liquid Aminos
¼ cup canola or olive oil

Directions

- Soak 4 ounces of Butler Soy Curls™ in 2–3 cups water for 10 minutes
- Sauté all vegetables and seasonings in oil in large skillet
- Add soaked soy curls and mix in with all other ingredients
- Cook on medium heat for another 10 minutes
- Serve with rice and peas or another favorite side dish and vegetables

Entrées

Arroz Con Curles des Soyas/Rice with Soy Curls

2 cups prepared soy curls
2 cups brown rice
1 cup chopped onion
1 cup chopped red sweet pepper
1 cup chopped green sweet pepper
1 cup chopped tomato
¼ cup garlic paste (4 cloves crushed garlic, 2 tablespoons olive oil, 2 tablespoons lemon juice)

2 tablespoons fresh parsley
1 tablespoon turmeric
1 tablespoon hot pepper sauce
½ cup olive oil
2 cups water
2 tablespoons Bragg Liquid Aminos

Directions

- Soak 1 cup soy curls in 1 cup water to get the 2 cups needed for the recipe
- Wash rice two or three times
- Sauté all vegetables and seasonings in oil in a skillet
- Add garlic paste and rice, then continue to stir
- Add water, pepper sauce, Bragg Liquid Aminos, and soy curls
- Mix together and allow to cook until rice is tender and liquid has been soaked up
- Serve with green salad or green beans

Curried Mushrooms and Soy Chips (or TVP)

2 pounds white or brown button mushrooms, sliced
1 ½ cups rehydrated soy chips or TVP
½ cup chopped onion
½ cup chopped red and green peppers
1 tablespoon chopped rosemary leaves
2 tablespoons curry powder
1 teaspoon hot pepper sauce (optional)
2 tablespoons Bragg Liquid Aminos
½ cup olive or canola oil
½ cup green and red pepper strips for garnish

Directions

- Put ¾ cup soy chips or TVP in 1 ½ cups warm water and soak for 10 minutes
- Wash, strip (optional), and slice mushrooms
- Heat oil and sauté mushrooms in large skillet, stirring for 5 minutes
- Add onions, other vegetables, and seasonings, and sauté for 5 more minutes
- Now add rehydrated soy chips (TVP) and mix well; continue to cook for 10–15 minutes
- Serve with rice and peas, seasoned bulgur, or another favorite side dish. Garnish with green and red pepper strips. May also serve on toast.

Entrées

Soy Curls and Ackee

8-ounce package Butler Soy Curls™
1 can ackee or 2 cups fresh ackee (where available)
1 cup chopped onion
3 cloves chopped garlic
2 cups chopped green, red, or yellow sweet peppers
1 medium chopped tomato
2 tablespoons chopped basil leaves
2 tablespoons thyme leaves
2 tablespoons curry powder
1 tablespoon Bragg Liquid Aminos
1 tablespoon hot pepper sauce (optional)
½ cup canola or olive oil
3–4 cups water for soaking soy curls

Directions

- Soak soy curls for 10 minutes
- Meanwhile, sauté all vegetables and seasonings, stirring gently
- Open can of ackee and drain the liquid; rinse the ackee carefully to prevent breaking
- Add soaked soy curls to vegetables in skillet; mix in gently and allow to cook for 10 minutes
- Mix in ackee, gently turning over with fork so it doesn't break up too much
- Simmer another 5 minutes
- Serve with steamed rice, yams/potatoes, mac n' cheese, boiled green bananas, or steamed breadfruit and dumplings

Variations with Soy Curls

- Use the following ingredient variations while following the above recipe for soy curls and ackee
    – Soy curls with shredded cabbage
    – Soy curls with carrots, green beans, and broccoli
    – Soy curls with collard greens; first steam collard greens until tender
    – Soy curls with stir-fried vegetables
    – Curried soy curls with cubed white potato

Tofu Logs in Coconut Sauce

1 package extra firm tofu
1 cup dried coconut
1 cup coconut milk
2 tablespoons lemon juice (optional)
¼ cup Sugar In The Raw® or 2 tablespoons blackstrap molasses or maple syrup
1 teaspoon ground nutmeg
1 teaspoon cinnamon powder
¼ cup fresh parsley leaves for garnish
½ teaspoon sea salt (optional)

Directions

- Drain water from tofu and cut tofu into strips 2 inches long by ¾ inches thick
- Put in deep dish for marinating
- Break coconut and remove the shell; cut in pieces and grate or put in chopper or blender and chop finely; or buy shredded coconut and blend it
- Mix together chopped coconut, coconut milk, spices, and sweetener
- Add ½ teaspoon sea salt (if desired)
- Add lemon juice (optional)
- Pour mixture on tofu logs and allow to marinate for 1–1 ½ hours
- Next, transfer to shallower baking dish and bake in oven for 30 minutes at 400 degrees F until most of the liquid is absorbed
- Remove from oven and garnish with parsley
- Serve with rice and beans, tomato slices, and coconut sauce (see recipe on page 81)

Entrées

Tofu Logs in Bar-B-Q Sauce

1 package extra firm tofu (USDA certified non-GMO)
1 cup homemade Bar-B-Q sauce (see recipe on page 80)

Directions

- Drain water from tofu and cut tofu into strips 2 inches long by ¾ inches thick
- Put tofu logs in baking dish and pour Bar-B-Q sauce on tofu
- Bake at 400 degrees F for 30 minutes
- Serve with your favorite side dish

Curried Tofu/Gluten Mince Scramble

1 package firm tofu
1 cup gluten mince (optional)
8-ounce package mushrooms
2 tablespoons curry powder
1–2 tablespoons chopped onions
1 teaspoon Italian seasoning

1 tablespoon Bragg Liquid Aminos
1–2 tablespoons chopped green/red peppers
1 teaspoon hot pepper sauce
½ cup chopped tomato
¼ cup canola or olive oil

Directions

- Crush tofu with egg crusher or fork
- Combine with gluten mince (see recipe on page 34)
- Wash, strip, and chop mushrooms
- Sauté onions, mushrooms, tofu/gluten mince in skillet
- Add tomato, curry powder, Italian seasoning, and salt
- Cook for 5–7 minutes while stirring with a fork
- Serve with brown rice, boiled potatoes and steamed vegetables (green beans or broccoli), seasoned bulgur wheat, dumplings, fried (or baked) ripe plantains, or tomatoes
- May also be served with grits as a breakfast dish or use it to make a sandwich

Entrées

Chickpea (Garbanzo) Rounds

2–3 cups mashed chickpeas (garbanzo beans)
½ cup finely chopped onions
½ cup chopped tomatoes
½ cup chopped celery
2 tablespoons chopped fresh or dried parsley
½ cup old fashioned oats
1 tablespoon cornstarch
½ cup whole wheat bread crumbs
½ cup almond or soy milk
2 tablespoons veggie soup base seasoning (see recipe on page 77)
2 tablespoons canola or olive oil
1 tablespoon light margarine (no dairy or eggs)
2 teaspoons Bragg Liquid Aminos

Directions

- Pour oil and margarine into a large skillet; melt the margarine
- Sauté onions, tomatoes, celery, and 1 tablespoon parsley; save 1 tablespoon parsley for garnish
- Add breadcrumbs, oats, and flour; mix well
- Add chickpeas (garbanzos) and all other ingredients and mix
- Form into rounds (patties) and bake in oiled baking pan; brown on both sides
- Serve on a bun with tomato, lettuce, and salsa or your favorite condiment

Hungry Man Veggie Wrap

Flatout® Flatbread, whole-grain flatbread, or Patty Shells (see recipe on page 57)

4 cups gluten strips, braised or curried (see recipe on page 34 or 35)

Or gluten roast slices or strips

Or curried seasoned soy curls (see recipe on page 38)

Or soy curl fritters

Or tofu scramble

Or tofu in coconut sauce

3 cups carrot curls, sweet pepper strips, tomato slices, and cucumber strips

Favorite sauce, dressing, or veggie cheese

Directions

- Make Patty Shells recipe and bake for 3 minutes or lay out purchased flatbread
- Place 1 cup of meat filling in center of wrap and top with ½–¾ cup vegetables and dressing
- Fold up about 1 inch of wrap from bottom
- Fold the right side of the wrap over the meat and vegetables and roll up; fasten with toothpick if desired

Entrées

Nut Curry

8 ounces chopped nuts
   (Brazil, cashew, walnuts)
¼ cup canola oil
2 large chopped onions
2 chopped apples
2 cups steamed brown rice
2 tablespoons rice flour or cornstarch
1 ½ tablespoons curry powder
2 tablespoons nutritional yeast
1 tablespoon Sugar In The Raw®
1 teaspoon Bragg Liquid Aminos or sea salt
2 tablespoons lemon juice
2 ½ cups water

Directions

- Wash apples, onions, and rice
- Chop apples and onions; grind nuts; steam rice in 2 cups water; and set aside
- Sauté onions and apples until tender
- Stir in curry powder, flour, and yeast flakes
- Add ½ cup water to sautéed mixture
- Bring to boil and cook until thickened, stirring constantly to prevent lumping; about 5 minutes
- Add nuts and all other ingredients, except rice, and mix well
- Continue to cook on low heat for another 2 minutes
- Serve over rice and vegetables; may serve with favorite sauce (optional)

Nut Loaf

2 cups gluten mince (see recipe on page 34)
1 cup old-fashioned oats
1 cup bread crumbs
½ cup peanut butter (omit if allergic)
½ cup ground walnuts
¼ cup ground flaxseed
¼ cup almond meal
½ cup nutritional yeast flakes
1 cup chopped green and red sweet peppers
1 chopped onion
½ cup grated carrots
1 tablespoon chopped basil
2 teaspoons Bragg Liquid Aminos
2 teaspoons hot pepper sauce
1 cup water

Directions
- Mix all ingredients together
- Pour into oiled baking dish
- Bake at 375 degrees F for 1–1 ½ hours
- Slice and serve with homemade Bar-B-Q sauce (see recipe on page 80)

Entrées

Rice and Nut Loaf

1 ½–2 cups precooked brown rice
1 cup shredded zucchini squash
½ cup finely chopped walnuts
½ cup wheat germ
½ cup pecan meal
½ cup chopped onion
¼ cup rice flour
1 cup cashew cheese sauce
  (see recipe on page 80)
1 tablespoon fresh thyme leaves
2 tablespoons fresh chopped basil
½ teaspoon marjoram
1 teaspoon hot pepper sauce

Directions

- Combine all ingredients and mix well
- Pour mixture into oiled 9-inch by 5-inch loaf pan
- Bake for 40-45 minutes at 350 degrees F or until golden brown; edges should by brown and firm to touch
- Cut into slices or 2-inch by 2-inch squares
- May serve hot or at room temperature with your favorite gravy

Sautéed Curried Lima Beans and Mushrooms

2 cups large frozen lima beans
1 medium diced tomato
1 pound fresh white or brown button mushrooms, washed, stripped (optional), and sliced
1 cup chopped green and red sweet peppers
1 medium chopped onion
1 tablespoon chopped fresh basil
1 tablespoon chopped rosemary
2 tablespoons curry powder
¼ cup veggie soup base seasoning
1 teaspoon Bragg Liquid Aminos or sea salt
¼ cup olive or canola oil

Directions

- Wash and prepare beans by steaming in 2 cups water for 10–15 minutes or until tender
- Wash and slice mushrooms
- Add oil to large skillet and heat on medium to high for 3 minutes
- Add the following ingredients to the skillet—lima beans, mushrooms, tomatoes, onions, peppers, basil, rosemary, and curry powder—and sauté for 5 minutes
- Add Bragg Liquid Aminos and soup base seasoning; mix and cook 10–15 minutes more
- Serve with steamed brown rice or steamed bulgur wheat or another favorite side dish

Split Peas and Nut Patties

- 1 cup cooked green or yellow split peas
- ½ cup almond meal
- ½ cup pecan meal
- ¼ cup peanut butter (omit if allergic)
- 1 ½ cups old-fashioned oats
- ½ cup rice flour
- ¼ cup veggie soup base seasoning (see recipe on page 77)
- ½ cup chopped onion
- ¾ cup chopped green and yellow sweet peppers
- 1 medium chopped tomato
- 1 tablespoon fresh chopped basil
- 1 tablespoon fresh chopped rosemary
- 2 teaspoons chopped garlic
- 2 teaspoons Bragg Liquid Aminos or sea salt
- 2 teaspoons browning
- 1 teaspoon hot pepper sauce

Directions

- Cook split peas in 2 cups water until tender
- Place all other ingredients into bowl and mix together
- Drain water from split peas and add peas to mixture in bowl and combine
- Form a ball or a log and cut into patties approximately 3 inches in diameter and ½ inch thick
- Lay patties on oiled baking sheet and bake at 375 degrees F for 20–25 minutes or until firm
- Serve on a roll with lettuce, tomato, etc.

Entrées

Vegan Nut Roast

1 cup mixed nuts
1 small chopped apple
½ cup rolled oats
1 tablespoon chopped sweet basil
½ cup chopped onions
½ cup chopped green/red peppers
½ cup chopped tomatoes
½ cup grated carrots
1 tablespoon veggie soup base seasoning (recipe on page 77)
¼ cup unbleached flour or cornstarch
½ cup almond milk or soymilk or water
1–2 teaspoons Bragg Liquid Aminos
1/3 cup canola or olive oil

Directions

- Grind mixed nuts and put in a mixing bowl with oatmeal and flour
- Heat oil and sauté onions, tomatoes, and apple until soft, then add chopped peppers and carrots
- Add oats, flour, and cornstarch to the nut mixture
- Add soup base seasoning
- Add milk or water and Bragg Liquid Aminos
- Mix all ingredients together
- Put in greased casserole dish or loaf tin
- Cover with foil and bake at 400 degrees F for 45 minutes–1 hour
- Remove foil and allow to brown for 5 minutes
- Serve with Brazil nut sauce (see recipe on page 80), with rice and vegetables, or as a sandwich

Vegan Meatloaf

3 cups gluten mince (see recipe on page 34) or soaked TVP
1 cup whole wheat bread crumbs
1 cup rolled oats
1 can chopped chestnuts (optional) or ½ cup peanut butter or almond butter
½ cup chopped onions
½ chopped green and red peppers
½ cup shredded carrots
2 tablespoons chopped parsley
2 tablespoons chopped basil
1 tablespoon chopped fresh rosemary
1 tablespoon fresh thyme leaves
1 teaspoon garlic powder
2 teaspoons hot pepper sauce (optional)
2 teaspoons Bragg Liquid Aminos or sea salt
1 tablespoon browning
1 cup almond milk
1 8-ounce can tomato sauce or homemade tomato sauce (6 tomatoes puréed)

Directions

- Preheat oven to 350 degrees F
- Combine all ingredients in bowl and mix well
- Scrape into 9-inch loaf tin or baking dish and bake for 35–45 minutes
- Slice or cut into 2-inch squares
- Serve with brown gravy (see recipe on page 79), steamed seasoned rice, bulgur wheat, couscous, or other side dishes, or use to make sandwiches

Entrées

Vegan/Vegetarian Meatballs

1 package firm tofu, mashed (USDA certified, non-GMO)
½ cup pecan meal
1 cup rolled oats
2 cups gluten flour
¾ cup nutritional yeast
3 tablespoons veggie soup base seasoning (see recipe on page 77)
¼ cup onion powder
1 tablespoon garlic powder
2 teaspoons chopped sage
1 tablespoons chopped dry basil
1 cup water
2 teaspoons Bragg Liquid Aminos or sea salt
6 cups tomato/spaghetti sauce
6 cups water
¾ cup canola oil for browning meatballs

Directions

- Mix all ingredients together, except the spaghetti sauce and water, to create a stiff mixture
- Roll into balls; 2 tablespoons of mix per meatball
- Brown meatballs in skillet in canola oil
- In large sauce pan/pot, put in spaghetti/tomato sauce and water and bring to a boil
- Add meatballs to the sauce and cook on medium heat for 1 ½–2 hours
- Serve on cooked whole wheat or rice spaghetti with vegetables

Vegan Squares

2 cups TVP
1 cup old-fashioned oats
½ cup whole wheat flour
1 cup whole wheat bread crumbs
1 cup almond meal
1 cup chopped tomato
1 cup chopped onion
1 cup chopped green/yellow sweet peppers
¼ cup nutritional yeast flakes
2 tablespoons Spanish thyme (if available) or dry thyme leaves
1 tablespoon chopped basil
1 teaspoon sage (optional)
2 teaspoons Bragg Liquid Aminos
½ cup canola or olive oil

Directions

- Soak TVP in 4 cups water
- Sauté all vegetables and seasonings in oil
- Add vegetables to first 5 ingredients and mix everything together
- Roll out on cutting board to ½-inch thick
- Cut into 2 inch squares
- Arrange on oiled baking sheet and bake at 350 degrees F for 20–30 minutes, brushing with oil to moisten
- Serve with favorite sauce or make into a sandwich with lettuce and tomato

Entrées

Veggie Casserole

2 cups soy curls
½ cup whole wheat flour or rice flour
1 cup chopped onions
1 cup sliced mushrooms
1 cup chopped green/red sweet peppers
1 cup chopped tomatoes
2 cups cut green beans
¼ cup chopped garlic
¼ cup chopped basil
1/8 cup thyme
½ cup cashew meal (optional)
½ cup sliced shallots, browned in 1 tablespoon oil
½ cup nutritional yeast flakes
1 cup almond milk
2 teaspoon Bragg Liquid Aminos
½ cup whole wheat seasoned breadcrumbs (no milk or eggs) or gluten-free breadcrumbs
1 cup water
½ cup olive oil
2 teaspoon hot pepper sauce (optional)

Directions

- Soak the soy curls with 2 tablespoons curry powder and 4 cups water
- Sauté the mushrooms, onions, garlic, peppers, basil, and thyme in oil
- Add flour and nutritional yeast and mix well
- Add milk, water, Bragg Liquid Aminos, and mix well
- Add soy curls and then mix well
- Add green beans, tomatoes, and carrots and mix together
- Put in oiled baking dish, top with breadcrumbs, and bake at 350 degrees F for 25 minutes until top is golden brown
- Remove and garnish with shallots
- Serve with boiled potatoes, steamed rice, or seasoned bulgur wheat

Vegekabob

1 cup potato cubes, bite size pieces
1 cup yellow/green squash cubes
1 cup green/red sweet peppers
1 cup broccoli spears
1 cup cherry tomatoes or cubed tomatoes
¼ cup veggie soup base seasoning
2 cups curried gluten bits
   (see recipe on page 36)

1 tablespoon curried pepper sauce
   (Jamaican style) or pickapeppa sauce
2 tablespoons onion powder
2 tablespoons chopped parsley
2 tablespoons Bragg Liquid Aminos
   or sea salt
1/3 cup lemon juice
½ cup canola or olive oil
Skewers, metal or bamboo

Directions
- Wash and cube vegetables in bite-size pieces
- Mix seasoning, soup base seasoning, lemon juice, Bragg Liquid Aminos, and oil
- Put all vegetables and gluten chick bites in seasoning mix and marinate for 15–20 minutes
- Alternate the gluten and vegetables on the skewers and cook on a grill, turning on all sides, about 5–10 minutes or bake skewers for 8–10 minutes, or until roasted, at 350 degrees F
- Serve with steamed rice or macaroni and cheese

Entrées

Carolle's Veggie Patty

Filling

- 3 cups gluten mince (see recipe on page 34) or TVP (1 ½ cups soaked in 3 cups water)
- ½ cup cooked bulgur wheat
- 1 cup finely chopped onion
- 1 cup chopped green, red, and yellow sweet peppers
- 1 medium chopped tomato
- 2 tablespoons chopped scallion
- 2 tablespoons chopped parsley
- 2 tablespoons fresh chopped basil
- 3 tablespoons curry powder
- 2 tablespoons onion powder
- 1 tablespoon garlic powder
- ¼ cup veggie soup base seasoning (see recipe on page 77)
- 1 tablespoon Bragg Liquid Aminos or 1 teaspoon sea salt (optional)
- ½ cup canola oil
- 1 cup whole wheat breadcrumbs

Directions

- Sauté all vegetables and seasonings in canola oil in a large skillet
- Add gluten mince or soaked TVP and bulgur wheat
- Mix together in skillet and cook for 20–30 minutes
- Add breadcrumbs, mix, and cook another 3–5 minutes
- Set aside while you make patty shells

Patty Shells

- 3 cups white whole wheat flour
- 1 cup rice or unbleached white flour
- 1 tablespoon turmeric powder
- 1 teaspoon sea salt (optional)
- 1 cup canola oil
- ¾ cup ice water

Directions

- Mix all dry ingredients in large mixing bowl
- Add oil to flour and mix in carefully; don't knead the dough
- Add enough water to make a firm dough that can be easily rolled out
- Form into a big ball, then cut into 3 smaller balls and stretch each log to 8 inches long and 2 inches thick
- Refrigerate dough for 15 minutes, then cut into 2-inch pieces, about 4 pieces per log
- On a floured cutting board with floured rolling pin, roll out each 2-inch piece into a thin layer and cut into a circle by using a saucer
- Spoon 2 tablespoons of filling into the center of the circle

- Fold the dough over the filling to form a crescent shape; fold edge of the dough under to secure the edge; seal edge by crimping with a fork
- Bake the patties at 350 degrees F for 30–35 minutes or until lightly brown
- Serve as a meal with a salad or as a snack, or make the patties smaller and serve as an appetizer

Entrées

Veggie Subway Pattie

1 cup soy curls broken into smaller pieces
½ cup crushed garbanzo beans
½ cup whole wheat flour or rice flour
½ cup old-fashioned oats
¼ cup nutritional yeast flakes
½ cup walnut or almond meal
1 cup chopped green and red sweet peppers
1 teaspoon chopped fresh or dried thyme
1 tablespoon chopped rosemary
1 finely chopped garlic clove
2 tablespoons curry powder
1 tablespoon onion powder
1 teaspoon Bragg Liquid Aminos
¾ cup almond milk
¼ cup canola oil (optional)

Directions

- Mix all ingredients together
- Form mixture into 3-inch by 2-inch by ¼-inch thick Subway-style burgers
- Heat 1 cup of canola oil in skillet and fry each burger until golden brown on each side or place burgers on a greased baking sheet, brushing each one with canola oil and bake until golden brown
- Serve with lettuce, tomatoes, sliced cucumbers, and your favorite dressing or sauce on a whole wheat sub or hoagie roll

Side Dishes

Jamaican-Style Rice and Red Beans

3 cups long grain brown rice
2 cups pre-soaked red beans or pigeon peas
2 cups coconut milk
4 cups water
1 small chopped onion
2 tablespoons fresh thyme leaves
2–3 stalks crushed and chopped scallions
1 tablespoon Bragg Liquid Aminos
　or 2 teaspoons sea salt
1 teaspoon hot pepper sauce (optional)

Directions

- Soak 1 cup dried beans in 3–4 cups of water for 2 hours or overnight and drain
- Wash rice 3 times, pouring off the water and removing any foreign particles
- In medium aluminum foil pan, put rice, 4 cups water, pre-soaked red beans and all other ingredients and mix well
- Cover the pan with aluminum foil
- Place in the oven at 350–400 degrees F for 1 ¼ hours or until rice and beans are tender and the water is absorbed
- Fluff with a fork and allow to steam for 15 more minutes
- Serve with your favorite entrée and vegetable

Seasoned Bulgur Wheat

2 cups cracked bulgur wheat
2 tablespoons light margarine
1 small finely chopped onion
2 teaspoons chopped parsley or basil
2 stalks finely chopped scallions
2 tablespoons chopped red peppers
2 teaspoons Bragg Liquid Aminos
4 cups water

Directions

- Bring water to a boil in a saucepan
- Wash bulgur wheat and remove any foreign particles
- Put bulgur and all ingredients in boiling water
- Decrease heat to medium low and cook until all the water is soaked up
- Fluff with a fork and serve with any favorite entrée
- Also use in making salads

Creamy Macaroni-n-Cheese

3 cups whole wheat or gluten-free macaroni
½ cup unsalted cashews
½ cup Goya coconut milk
½ cup nutritional yeast flakes
2–3 teaspoons Bragg Liquid Aminos
2 teaspoons onion powder

1 teaspoon garlic powder
½ cup cornstarch
2 cups water
½ cup pimentos or 2 teaspoons turmeric
3–4 tablespoons lemon juice

Directions

- Put 6 cups water in a large pot and bring to a boil with 1 teaspoon salt; once boiling add macaroni and allow to cook until tender
- Remove from stove and strain off hot water; then set aside in pot
- Wash cashews and put in a blender with all other ingredients; blend until creamy and smooth
- Add sauce to macaroni and mix carefully
- Pour in large baking dish and bake for 20 minutes at 375 degrees F or cook for 10 minutes on top of the stove until thickened
- Serve with vegetables

Side Dishes

Baked Sweet Potato (Yam) Wedges

3 large yellow sweet potatoes (yams)
2 tablespoons light margarine or ¼ cup canola oil
1 tablespoon ground nutmeg or cinnamon (optional)

Directions

- Wash very well; remove skin if desired
- Cut lengthwise in 1-inch thick wedges
- Arrange potato wedges on oiled baking sheet
- Dot with pieces of margarine or brush oil on each wedge
- Sprinkle with nutmeg or cinnamon (optional)
- Cover with foil and bake for 15 minutes at 375 degrees F
- Remove foil and continue baking 15–20 minutes or until brown and crispy
- Eat as an appetizer or side dish like French fries

Healthful Living Cookbook

Candied Sweet Potatoes with Orange Slices

2 pounds yellow sweet potatoes (yams)
2 tablespoons light margarine
2 tablespoons cinnamon powder
2 tablespoons ground nutmeg
½ cup maple syrup
   or ¼ cup Sugar In The Raw®
1 or 2 oranges
2 cups orange juice
1–2 cups water

Directions

- Wash sweet potatoes, scrape or peel skin; cut into ½-inch thick slices, strips, or quarters
- Wash oranges; slice thinly and then cut into halves
- Pour water into large baking dish and lay the potatoes in the dish
- Sprinkle with the spices and drizzle on maple syrup or sprinkle on Sugar-in-the-Raw®
- Dot with margarine pieces
- Pour on orange juice
- Lay orange slices on top of potatoes
- Place baking dish in 350-degree F oven and cover with foil for first 15 minutes; then remove foil and continue baking for 20–30 minutes or until tender

Dr. U's Potato Salad

3 cups cooked, peeled, diced white and yellow (sweet) potatoes
½ cup finely chopped green and red peppers
½ cup sweet peas
¼ cup finely chopped onion
1 teaspoon sea salt (optional)
1 tablespoon chopped parsley
1 cup vegan mayonnaise
   (see recipe on page 78)

Directions

- Combine cooked, diced potatoes with all vegetables and seasonings, except parsley, and gently mix in a large bowl
- Add the vegan mayonnaise and gently mix again
- Scrape into salad bowl and sprinkle parsley flakes on top as garnish

Side Dishes

Nadia's Potato and Green Bean Salad

2 pounds of small red skin potatoes or golden potatoes
1 pound frozen green beans
4 finely chopped garlic cloves
2 teaspoons black pepper (optional)
2 teaspoons salt
½ cup chopped cilantro
3 tablespoons extra virgin olive oil
1 medium lemon
1 medium/large bowl of ice water

Directions
- First, thoroughly clean the potatoes, including the skin
- Cut potatoes in half or if large cut in quarters
- Bring a large pot of water to boil and place the green beans into the pot of boiling water for 1 minute; then remove them and place in a bowl of ice water to stop the cooking process and keep them green
- Place the potatoes into the boiling water once the green beans are removed
- In a separate bowl, combine lemon juice, salt, pepper, and garlic; then slowly whisk in olive oil and set dressing mixture aside
- Once the potatoes are fully cooked, drain and put the potatoes into a large bowl
- Add the green beans to the bowl with the potatoes
- Pour the dressing over the potatoes and beans and lightly toss
- Put potato salad in refrigerator to chill, then serve; may also be served as warm potato salad

Healthful Living Cookbook

Carolle's Pasta Salad

1 pound whole wheat (no milk or eggs) or rice pasta rotini
2 cups of three bean salad
1 small finely chopped onion
2 medium chopped tomatoes
1 chopped cucumber
1 cup homemade lemon/oil dressing or fat-free Italian dressing
1 tablespoon chopped parsley for garnish

Directions

- Cook the pasta and set aside
- Make homemade three bean salad by mixing together 1 cup pre-cooked red beans, cut green beans, and wax beans, ¼ cup lemon juice, and ¼ cup olive oil or canola oil
- Mix all ingredients together in a large mixing bowl
- Make salad dressing, which follows, and pour over the pasta salad:
  - ½ cup lemon juice
  - ½ cup olive or canola oil
  - 2 teaspoons Bragg Liquid Aminos or sea salt
  - 2 teaspoons onion powder
  - 1 teaspoon garlic powder
  - ½ teaspoon celery salt
  - 2 teaspoons dried basil
- Garnish the finished salad with parsley
- May add your favorite nuts or cubed veggie meat to the dish

Baked Ripe Sweet Plantain

2 whole yellow ripe (sweet) plantains
¼ cup canola oil

Directions

- Wash ripe (sweet) plantains, remove the skin, and slice in 2 halves lengthwise, and then cut across in 3 pieces
- Pour canola oil in medium-sized aluminum foil pan
- Lay plantain pieces in pan and brush tops with oil from pan
- Bake at 350 degrees F for 20–25 minutes or until golden brown
- Serve as a side dish with tofu scramble for breakfast or at dinner with any entrée, another side dish, and vegetables

Side Dishes

Steamed Breadfruit with Rosemary

½ of one breadfruit
2 cups water
4 tablespoons light margarine

1 tablespoon onion powder
½ teaspoon sea salt (optional)
1 tablespoon chopped fresh or dried rosemary

Directions

- Buy one whole, mature (not soft) breadfruit; wash and cut into two halves lengthwise
- Cut one half of the breadfruit into 4–6 equal slices
- Remove the core, then peel the green skin from each slice with a knife
- Wash the slices
- Pour 2 cups of water in a large skillet and bring to a boil; add margarine
- Lay each slice of breadfruit in skillet and sprinkle with rosemary
- Cover and lower heat to medium
- Allow breadfruit to steam until soft and firm like a cooked white potato when poked with a fork
- Serve with your favorite entrée and vegetables

Soups

Carolle's Cream of Pumpkin Soup

4 cups diced pumpkin, peeled
1 cup chopped onion
1 cup chopped celery
½ cup chopped green onions
1 cup diced carrots
½ cup canola/olive oil
1 teaspoon pepper sauce
1 tablespoon Bragg Liquid Aminos
1–2 cups coconut milk
4 cups vegetable stock

Directions
- In a large skillet, sauté diced pumpkin and all vegetables in oil for 5 minutes
- Add stock, Bragg Liquid Aminos, and pepper sauce and continue to cook another 10 minutes
- Pour in blender and purée until smooth
- Add coconut milk and return to fire
- Simmer for 5 additional minutes
- Serve in small bowls with small dumpling twists

Stock

1 cup chopped celery
2 cups chopped carrots
1 cup chopped onions
¼ cup canola oil
1 tablespoon thyme leaves
1 tablespoon chopped basil
6 cups water

- Put all ingredients in large stockpot and boil for 15–20 minutes.

Little Dumpling Twists

1 cup whole wheat flour or rice flour
¼ cup water

- Mix flour and water until it forms a dough
- Cut into small pieces and roll out, then twist and cook in the soup

Mixed Beans and Vegetable Combo

1 cup red kidney beans
1 cup white (cannellini) beans
1 cup frozen lima beans
1 cup carrot chunks or strips
1 cup chopped white button mushrooms
1 chopped onion
2–3 stalks chopped green onions (scallion)
1 pressed and chopped garlic clove
1 cup chopped sweet peppers
  (red, green, yellow)
1 diced tomato
½ cup chopped celery
1 tablespoon fresh or dried thyme leaves
2 bay leaves
2 tablespoons chopped cilantro
¼ cup veggie soup base seasoning
1 medium sweet potato cut in bite-size pieces
1 cup tomato sauce
  (original or garlic and herbs)
2 teaspoons Bragg Liquid Aminos or sea salt
¼ cup olive or canola oil
¼ cup fresh or dried chopped parsley (for garnish)
4 cups hot water

Directions

- Pour 2 cups of water into a large saucepan
- Cook lima beans and sweet potato for 15 minutes
- Add red and white beans to pan; decrease heat to medium while cooking
- Sauté mushrooms, onions, garlic, green onions, celery, tomatoes, cilantro, sweet peppers, and bay leaves in oil for 10 minutes
- Add the 4 cups hot water and all other ingredients to saucepan with beans
- Cover and continue to cook on medium heat for 10–15 minutes until vegetables and beans are tender and combo is tasty
- Serve in warm soup bowls with crackers or rolls; garnish soup with parsley

Soups

Red or Pink Beans Soup

2 cups dried red or pink kidney beans
6 cups water for soaking beans
1 cup chopped onion
2 stalks chopped green onions (scallion)
1 cup chopped red, green, and yellow sweet peppers
1 cup diced carrots
1 cup diced tomatoes
1 cup sliced or cubed cho-cho (chayotes) (small light green squash)
2–3 white potatoes cut in chunks
1 tablespoon fresh or dried thyme leaves
2 teaspoons hot pepper sauce
¼ cup veggie soup base seasoning
2 teaspoons Bragg Liquid Aminos or sea salt
2 cups coconut milk
6 cups water for soup
1 cup rice flour for dumplings (optional)

Directions

- Wash dried beans and remove any foreign particles; soak beans in 6 cups of water for 3–4 hours or overnight; after soaking, pour out the water and drain the beans
- Wash all other vegetables before chopping
- In large saucepan or pot, bring the 6 cups of water for the soup to boil
- Add soaked beans, coconut milk, cho-cho, potatoes, soup base seasoning, and Bragg Liquid Aminos to boiling water and cook on medium/high heat until beans are quite tender
- Add all other seasonings and vegetables; continue cooking for 10 minutes
- If desired, make dumplings using rice flour mixed with ½ cup of water; mix into a firm dough and break off small pieces about the size of your index finger and add to soup
- Continue cooking on medium heat for 15 more minutes
- When soup is ready, serve as a whole meal with bread or crackers

Salads and Vegetable Dishes

Multi-mix Vegetable Salad

1 head romaine lettuce
2 cups spinach leaves
1 cup sliced red and green sweet peppers
1 cup sliced tomatoes or grape tomatoes
1 cup broccoli spears
1 cup sliced yellow squash
1 cup bean sprouts

Directions

- Wash all vegetables and then cut them into bite-sized pieces
- Mix all vegetables in a large salad bowl
- Serve with your favorite dressing

Tabbouleh Salad on Romaine Lettuce

2 cups bulgur wheat
2 tablespoons light margarine
2 teaspoons Bragg Liquid Aminos or sea salt
2 medium chopped tomatoes
1 medium chopped cucumber
1 medium chopped onion
2 tablespoons chopped fresh or dried parsley
1 pressed and chopped garlic clove
½ cup lemon juice
½ cup olive or canola oil
1 teaspoon hot pepper sauce (optional)
2-3 cups chopped romaine lettuce

Directions

- Wash bulgur and remove any foreign particles; then drain off the water
- In a saucepan, pour in 2 cups of water and bring to a boil. Add 1 teaspoon Bragg Liquid Aminos or sea salt and margarine
- Add bulgur to boiling water; stir and reduce heat to low and let stand for 15–20 minutes until water is absorbed. Fluff with a fork.
- Put bulgur in refrigerator for about 10 minutes to cool; then remove and add vegetables, oil, lemon juice, seasonings, last amount of Bragg Liquid Aminos and pepper sauce
- Mix all ingredients together in a salad bowl
- Serve on a bed of lettuce; this is a complete meal

Oven Roasted Brussels Sprouts

24 small green Brussels sprouts
2 tablespoons onion powder
1 tablespoon garlic salt
2 tablespoons light margarine
2 tablespoons chopped rosemary

Directions
- Wash Brussels sprouts carefully
- Put all Brussels sprouts in a baking dish, sprinkle with all of the seasonings and margarine
- Roast in oven until browned
- Serve with favorite side dish and entrée or with cashew sauce (see recipe on page 80)

Seasoned Collard Greens with Soy Chips

2 pounds chopped fresh collard greens
1 cup soaked soy chips (chicken style) or soy curls
2 tablespoons chopped onion
1 tablespoon chopped garlic
1 cup chopped red and green sweet peppers
1 tablespoon Bragg Liquid Aminos
¼ cup canola or olive oil
Pepper to taste (optional)
½ cup water

Directions
- Sauté onions, peppers, and garlic in oil with Bragg Liquid Aminos
- Add collard greens and soy chips or soy curls
- Add water, then cover and steam until tender
- Serve with rice and peas, etc.

Salads and Vegetable Dishes

Cauliflower Steak with Curry Sauce

2 large cauliflower steaks (sliced from large cauliflower)
2 teaspoons onion powder
1 teaspoon garlic salt
1 tablespoon finely chopped basil
2 tablespoons parsley flakes
¼ cup canola or olive oil

Curry Sauce

2 tablespoons curry powder
2 tablespoons cornstarch
2 teaspoons onion powder
½ teaspoon Bragg Liquid Aminos or sea salt
¾ cup water
1 tablespoon light margarine
2 tablespoons chopped red sweet pepper

Directions

- Slice two or more large steaks by starting at the top center of the cauliflower head and cutting toward the bottom of the stalk; cut about ½- to 1-inch-thick slices
- Wash steaks and dry with paper towel
- Season with onion powder, garlic salt, and basil
- Put steaks in oiled skillet and sear until brown on both sides
- Remove to serving dish and sprinkle with parsley
- Make the curry sauce by mixing all ingredients together in a skillet and cooking until thickened
- Serve the cauliflower steaks with curry sauce and rice, seasoned bulgur wheat, or pasta

Baked Eggplant with Onions, Tomatoes, and Cashew Cheese Sauce

2 medium-sized firm eggplants
2 large sliced onions
2 large diced tomatoes
1 chopped green pepper
2 mashed and chopped garlic cloves
2 tablespoons chopped fresh basil
2 teaspoons hot pepper sauce

¼ cup nutritional yeast flakes
2 teaspoons Bragg Liquid Aminos or sea salt
¼ cup olive oil or canola oil
½ cup cashew cheese sauce
  (see recipe on page 80)
½ cup homemade bread crumbs

Directions

- Wash eggplants in cool salt water and let stand for 15–20 minutes; then dry and cut in four halves
- Wash tomatoes, onions, and fresh seasonings
- In a large skillet, pour oil and heat on medium-high heat
- Place cut side of eggplant in hot oil and sear; then drain oil onto wax paper and place eggplant halves in baking dish or pan
- Sauté all vegetables and seasonings for 8–10 minutes until tender
- Spread a spoonful of sautéed mixture on each half of eggplant in baking dish
- Top with cashew cheese sauce and sprinkle with a small amount of breadcrumbs
- Bake at 350 degrees F until golden brown, about 20–30 minutes
- May serve with rolls or pita bread

Soup Bases and Sauces

Veggie Soup Base/Seasoning

2 cups nutritional yeast flakes
2 tablespoons onion powder
1 tablespoon garlic powder
1 tablespoon celery salt
1 teaspoon sage
1 tablespoon dried basil

3 tablespoons parsley flakes
1 tablespoon turmeric powder
   or 1 teaspoon curry powder
2 teaspoons brown Sugar In The Raw®
1 teaspoon dry thyme leaves

Directions

- In food processor or coffee grinder, grind all ingredients until fine and well blended
- Store in a tightly covered jar
- You may make large amounts of soup base by doubling or tripling the recipe
- Use for seasoning meats, salads, soups, or any recipe

Homemade Tomato-Basil Dressing

2 medium tomatoes
1 tablespoon chopped basil
¼ cup olive oil

¼ cup lemon juice
1 crushed garlic clove
1 teaspoon Bragg Liquid Aminos

Directions

- Deseed tomatoes
- Blend all ingredients together
- Pour into salad dressing decanter
- Refrigerate after use

Lemon-Garlic Dressing

½ cup lemon juice
½ cup olive oil
½ teaspoon Bragg Liquid Aminos
1 teaspoon fresh basil
1 crushed garlic clove
1 teaspoon onion powder

Directions

- Put all ingredients in blender and blend for 1 minute
- Store in refrigerator

Vegan Mayonnaise

3 cups water
¼ cup fresh lemon juice
½ cup unsalted cashews
1 tablespoon onion powder
2 teaspoons garlic powder
2–3 teaspoons Bragg Liquid Aminos
¼ cup canola or olive oil
½ cup cornstarch

Directions

- Bring all ingredients to a boil except lemon juice and oil; turn heat to medium-low and simmer, stirring constantly to prevent lumps until thickened
- Transfer mixture to blender
- Add oil and lemon juice while blending
- Pour into a jar and allow to cool; label and date
- Use like mayonnaise in salads, sandwiches, and dips

Soup Bases and Sauces

Brown Gravy

1 cup rice flour
2 tablespoons light margarine
½ cup finely chopped onion
2 finely crushed garlic cloves
1 tablespoon veggie soup base seasoning

2 cups water
2 tablespoons Bragg Liquid Aminos
1 teaspoon pepper sauce
½ teaspoon browning

Directions

- Add flour and margarine to a skillet and stir constantly for 3–5 minutes over low-medium heat
- Add onion, garlic, and pepper to flour mixture
- Add soup base seasoning and mix
- Add water, Bragg Liquid Aminos, and browning; mix gently and stir constantly to prevent lumps from forming
- Use with meats and other dishes as needed

Brazil Nut Sauce

2 cups water
½ cup Brazil nuts
3 tablespoons veggie soup base seasoning (see recipe on page 77)
2 tablespoons chopped onion
1 chopped garlic clove
1 tablespoon celery salt
½ cup cornstarch
1 teaspoon Bragg Liquid Aminos

Directions
- Blend all ingredients together until smooth
- Bring mixture to a boil, stirring constantly, until thickened and without lumps

Homemade Bar-B-Q Sauce

1 cup chopped onion
2 crushed garlic cloves
3 cups tomato sauce
½ cup maple syrup
½ cup molasses
1 tablespoon sea salt (optional)
2 tablespoons canola oil

Directions
- Sauté onions and garlic in a skillet
- Add all other ingredients and simmer for 20–30 minutes
- Refrigerate and use as needed

Cashew Cheese Sauce

1 cup raw cashews
2 ½ cups coconut milk
1 ½ tablespoons onion powder
½ teaspoon garlic powder
¾ cup nutritional yeast flakes
½ cup cornstarch or rice flour
2 teaspoons Bragg Liquid Aminos or sea salt
2 cups water
¼ cup lemon juice
2 tablespoons turmeric powder

Directions
- Put all ingredients, except lemon juice, into a blender and blend until very smooth
- Pour into saucepan and bring to a boil, stirring constantly on medium heat to prevent lumping
- Add lemon juice and continue to cook for 1 minute longer, stirring well
- May store in glass container for about 2 weeks in refrigerator; may also freeze in glass container, ¾ full, or in a freezer bag (labeled and dated)
- If you don't have cashews, you may use walnuts or pecans

Soup Bases and Sauces

Coconut Sauce with Zing

3 cups coconut milk
1 tablespoon Sugar In The Raw®
1 tablespoon grated ginger or lemon juice
1 tablespoon cinnamon powder
1 tablespoon ground vanilla beans

Directions

- Pour coconut milk in a medium saucepan
- Add sugar and spices and stir well
- Allow to cook and reduce to about 1 ½ cups

Carolle's Fresh Fruit Sauce

1 cup black or green grapes
1 cup halved strawberries
1 cup pineapple chunks or one 8-ounce can pineapple tidbits with juice
1 tablespoon vanilla
1 tablespoon cinnamon powder
1 tablespoon ground nutmeg
½ cup apple juice
¼ cup cornstarch

Directions

- Put all ingredients in a saucepan
- Bring to a boil; then let simmer on medium heat until reduced and thickened

Spicy Homemade Hummus

2–3 cups cannellini beans or garbanzo beans
2 tablespoons veggie soup base seasoning (see recipe on page 77)
1 tablespoon onion powder or ¼ cup chopped onion
1 tablespoon garlic powder or 2 chopped garlic cloves
1 teaspoon hot pepper sauce
¼ cup lemon juice
2 teaspoons Bragg Liquid Aminos
2 tablespoons canola or olive oil

Directions
- Put all ingredients in a blender and blend until smooth and creamy
- Use as a dip or as a sandwich base/spread

Soup Bases and Sauces

Cashew Cheese Spread or Dip

½ cup raw cashews
1 cup nutritional yeast flakes
½ cup cornstarch
2 teaspoons onion powder
1 teaspoon garlic powder
¼ cup pimentos or 2 tablespoons turmeric powder
2 teaspoons Bragg Liquid Aminos
3 cups water
¼ cup lemon juice

Directions

- Blend all ingredients together, except lemon juice, until smooth
- Cook on medium heat for 10 minutes
- Add lemon juice and allow to thicken, stirring constantly

Lemon-Ackee/Coconut Sauce

1 can ackee in brine
1 ½ cups coconut milk
1 tablespoon lemon juice
½–1 teaspoon hot pepper sauce (optional)
½ teaspoon Bragg Liquid Aminos or sea salt
4 teaspoons grated lemon rind
2 tablespoons curry powder
2 tablespoons cornstarch or rice flour
¼ cup chopped onion
1 tablespoon chopped fresh or dried basil
½ teaspoon garlic powder
2 tablespoons nutritional yeast flakes
2 tablespoons canola oil

Directions

- Sauté onion and parsley in a skillet for 2 minutes
- Remove from heat and add to a blender, along with the following ingredients: ackee (drained and washed), lemon rind, garlic powder, curry powder, cornstarch (or rice flour), Bragg Liquid Aminos, pepper sauce; blend until smooth
- Pour mixture into saucepan and bring to boil on medium heat, whisking or stirring constantly to prevent lumping; cook for about 5 minutes
- Add lemon juice and cook for 1 minute more
- Serve over steamed rice, seasoned bulgur wheat, or steamed veggies

Peanut Butter Almond Sauce

1 cup almond milk
1 tablespoon light margarine
2 tablespoons rice flour
½ teaspoon Bragg Liquid Aminos
2 tablespoons peanut butter

Directions

- Warm milk in a saucepan on medium-low heat
- Melt margarine in another small saucepan; blend in flour and Bragg Liquid Aminos
- Combine margarine mixture with milk and stir constantly to prevent lumps until thickened
- Add peanut butter or other nut butter if allergic to peanuts and whisk until smooth
- Use on different veggie meats, meat loaf, or nut roasts, or use as a spread or dip

Carrot and Beet Sauce or Spread

1 cup chopped carrots
1 cup peeled and chopped beets
1 cup chopped watercress or lettuce
½ cup butternut squash or cucumber
¼ cup flaxseed oil or olive oil

½ cup lemon juice
2 teaspoons Bragg Liquid Aminos or sea salt
1 tablespoon onion powder
¼ cup cornstarch
1 teaspoon hot pepper sauce

Directions

- Blend all ingredients together in a blender, except lemon juice
- Put mixture in a saucepan and boil on medium heat for 5 minutes, stirring constantly to prevent lumps
- Add lemon juice and continue cooking for 1–2 minutes while stirring
- Makes a nice dressing, dip, or spread

Parsley/Cilantro Sauce

1 cup chopped parsley/cilantro
½ cup raw cashews
¼ cup lemon juice
1 pressed garlic clove

1 tablespoon onion powder
1 teaspoon Bragg Liquid Aminos or sea salt
1 teaspoon hot pepper sauce (optional)

Directions

- Blend all ingredients until smooth
- Serve with steamed rice or pasta dishes
- Store in dressing flask, labeled and dated

Homemade Block Cheese (Cashew, Pecan or Walnut)

1 cup cashews, pecans, or walnut
¾ cup nutritional yeast flakes
1/3 cup cornstarch or rice flour
2 teaspoons Bragg Liquid Aminos

¼ cup pimentos or
  2 tablespoons turmeric powder
1/3 cup lemon juice
3 cups water

Directions

- Blend all ingredients until very smooth and creamy
- Cook in saucepan, whisking constantly for 2–3 minutes, until thickened
- Use as a spread and store in the refrigerate or freeze and slice (remove from freezer and allow to thaw a little before slicing)

Bread, Biscuits

Ezekiel Bread (Without Yeast)

2 cups warm water
2 cups whole wheat ground
2 cups barley ground
1 cup cooked and ground white beans
1 cup cooked and ground lentils
1 cup cooked millet
2 tablespoons olive oil
½ cup seeds (fennel or poppy)
1 ½ teaspoons sea salt (optional)

Directions

- Add salt (if desired) to water
- Add all ingredients, except seeds
- Beat vigorously for 1 minute
- Allow to stand for 5–6 minutes
- Knead dough for 5 minutes on a lightly floured table; pinch and knead to get out air
- Cover for 30 minutes
- Then shape into a loaf and sprinkle with seeds
- Put dough into a greased loaf tin and bake at 350 degrees F for 30–40 minutes or until lightly golden brown
- Remove from loaf tin and allow to cool

Nadia's Biscuits

2 cups all-purpose flour, whole wheat flour, or rice flour
2 tablespoons Sugar In The Raw®
2 teaspoons baking powder
3 tablespoons light margarine
A pinch of iodized salt
1 cup water
1 cup canola oil for frying

Directions

- Mix flour, sugar, baking powder, and salt together in a large bowl
- Add in the margarine, cutting it into the flour or breaking it up piece by piece into the flour mixture with your clean hands, leaving chunks of margarine throughout
- Briefly mix together with your hand, being sure not to over mix
- Slowly add water to the bowl and mix together until it forms into a large piece of dough, again being sure not to over mix

- Put oil in a frying pan and turn the stove on medium high
- Break off a piece of dough to form small- to medium-sized balls by rolling the dough between both hands, then flatten them slightly in between both hands and place in the oil one by one
- When the biscuit turns golden brown, flip over to the other side, making sure that both sides are golden brown
- Once the biscuit is golden brown on both sides, remove from frying pan and place onto a plate lined with a paper towel to soak up the excess oil

Oatmeal/Coconut Biscuits

1 cup ground old-fashioned oats
½ cup coconut milk
½ cup whole wheat or rice flour
½ teaspoon sea salt (optional)
¼ cup water (if necessary)
4 tablespoons canola or olive oil

Directions

- Mix all ingredients, including 2 tablespoons of the oil, together in mixing bowl to make a stiff dough
- Roll out dough to ¼-inch thick on an oiled baking sheet
- Cut in 2-inch squares
- Bake for 20 minutes at 350 degrees F
- Use with any dip or eat plain or with fruit sauce

Desserts

Apple-Raisin Millet Cake

2 cups apple or pineapple juice
1 cup finely chopped apples or 1 cup crushed pineapple
1 cup chopped raisins
1 cup millet flour
1 cup self-rising unbleached white flour
½ teaspoon sea salt
1 tablespoon cinnamon
1 tablespoon grated nutmeg
1 teaspoon ground vanilla beans

Directions

- Wash and finely chop apples
- Mix all ingredients together in a large saucepan
- Cover and simmer on medium heat for 20–25 minutes, stirring to prevent lumps
- Pour into greased loaf tin and bake in oven for 10–15 minutes at 350 degrees F or until golden brown
- Cool and serve with ice cream or fruit preserves

Vegan Dump Cake

2 cups fresh chopped apples, strawberries, peaches, raisins, and crushed pineapple
½ cup crushed walnuts or almonds
1 cup white whole wheat flour or rice flour
2 teaspoons baking powder
½ cup coconut milk
½ cup almond milk
1 tablespoon cinnamon
1 tablespoon grated nutmeg
1 tablespoon melted margarine
¼ cup maple syrup
¼ cup grated or blended coconut flesh for topping
2 cups crushed graham crackers
1 teaspoon salt (optional)

Directions

- Mix together crushed graham crackers and melted margarine in a bowl; make sure the graham crackers do not have cow's milk or eggs in the ingredient list
- Press crushed graham crackers mixture onto the bottom and around the sides of a 9-inch baking tin
- Mix all other ingredients, except coconut topping, with milk and pour into baking tin
- Bake at 375 degrees F for 50–60 minutes; top with coconut after 40 minutes in the oven
- Serve with fruit sauce (see recipe on page 81)

Carolle's Sweet Potato Pie

3 cups cooked, mashed sweet potatoes
1 tablespoon cinnamon powder
1 tablespoon ground or grated nutmeg
1 tablespoon ground vanilla beans
1 teaspoon sea salt (optional)

½ cup whole wheat flour or cornstarch
½ cup Sugar In The Raw®
1 tablespoon melted margarine
2–3 cups crushed graham crackers

Directions

- Wash and cook sweet potatoes in skin
- Put in cold water to help remove skin easier, and then mash the potatoes
- Mix all dry ingredients together, except graham crackers
- Put mashed potatoes in a bowl and add spice and flour mixture; mix thoroughly to avoid lumps
- Mix together crushed graham crackers and melted margarine in a bowl; make sure the graham crackers do not have cow's milk or eggs in the ingredient list
- Press crushed graham crackers mixture onto the bottom and around the sides of a 9-inch baking tin
- Fill pie crust with mashed potato mixture
- Bake at 350 degrees F for 15–20 minutes
- Serve with favorite homemade ice cream

Desserts

Cornmeal Pudding with Almond-Coconut Sauce

2 cups medium ground yellow cornmeal
1 teaspoon baking powder
½ teaspoon sea salt (optional)
1 tablespoon powdered vanilla beans
1 tablespoon ground nutmeg
1 tablespoon cinnamon powder

1 cup chopped raisins
2 ½ cups almond milk
  (or other nut or soy milk)
3 ½ cups coconut milk
½ cup Sugar In The Raw® or maple syrup

Sauce
½ cup almond milk
½ cup coconut milk
¼ cup Sugar In The Raw® or maple syrup
½ tablespoon powdered vanilla beans
½ tablespoon ground nutmeg
½ tablespoon cinnamon powder

Directions

- Mix all dry ingredients together in large bowl: cornmeal, baking powder, spices, and salt
- Pour 2 ½ cups almond milk, 3 ½ cups coconut milk and sugar or maple syrup into a saucepan and mix to dissolve sugar
- Add cornmeal mixture and raisins to milk mixture
- Using a whisk, mix constantly and carefully to prevent lumps
- Cook pudding mixture on top of stove for 5–8 minutes or until it thickens
- Pour half-cooked pudding into greased baking tin
- Bake for 40–45 minutes at 375 degrees F
- After 10 minutes, pour ½ cup of sauce mixture on top of pudding
- When there is only 10 minutes left, pour on the rest of the sauce and finish baking
- Serve warm or chill and serve cold

Sweet Potato Pudding

4 cups grated or puréed white sweet potatoes
2 cups unbleached white or rice flour
2 cups chopped or whole raisins
1 whole dry coconut
1 ½ cups Sugar In The Raw®
1 ½ tablespoons ground vanilla beans
2 tablespoons cinnamon powder
2 tablespoons grated or powdered nutmeg
2 ½ cups almond milk
4 cups coconut milk
1 teaspoon sea salt (optional)

Directions

- Put sweet potatoes, flour, and raisins in a large bowl and mix
- Break coconut and remove flesh from hard shell; wash and cut flesh in small pieces, then grate or purée in blender
- Mix puréed coconut in bowl with potato mixture
- Mix liquids, spices, and sugar together with a whisk; set aside 1 cup liquid mixture to use as topping
- Pour milk mixture into potato mixture and mix well
- Pour finished mixture into a greased 10-inch baking pan until it is ¾ full
- Bake in oven at 375–400 degrees F for 60 minutes
- After 10 minutes, pour half of topping on pudding and continue baking
- After 30 minutes, pour remainder of topping on pudding and bake for 20 minutes longer
- Remove from oven and serve warm or cold

Desserts

Fruit and Nut Bread Pudding

4–6 cups cubed whole wheat or gluten-free bread
½ pound firm tofu
1 cup almond meal or chopped almonds
1 cup chopped ripe bananas or diced cherries or raisins
1 ½ cups coconut milk
1 ½ cups almond or soy milk
½ cup Sugar In The Raw® or organic sugar
3–4 teaspoons alcohol-free vanilla or 2 teaspoons ground vanilla beans
1 tablespoon cinnamon powder
1 tablespoon ground or grated nutmeg
½ teaspoon sea salt (optional)
2 tablespoons light margarine

Directions

- Mix bread and almond meal/chopped almonds, cinnamon, and nutmeg in mixing bowl
- In another bowl, combine milk, vanilla, tofu, and sugar and purée in blender for 2 minutes
- Pour liquid mixture on bread mixture; add fruit and mix thoroughly
- Pour full mixture into an oiled baking dish and bake at 350 degrees F for 1–1 ½ hours
- Serve with a sauce or homemade ice cream

Cherry Sauce

1 cup almond milk
1 tablespoon Sugar In The Raw®
4 cups chopped cherries
1 teaspoon nutmeg
1 teaspoon cinnamon
2 teaspoons alcohol-free vanilla

Directions

- In a small saucepan, bring all sauce ingredients to boil and simmer for 6 minutes while stirring
- Serve on top of bread pudding, hot or chilled

Carolle's Fresh Tropical Fruit Salad

2 ripe bananas
½ cup orange juice
1–2 medium ripe mangos
2 cups fresh pineapple chunks
1 cup fresh strawberries

2 ripe naseberries, if available (see glossary) or 2 flat persimmons
2 cups grated coconut flesh for garnish
2 cups fresh fruit sauce
 (see recipe on page 81)

Directions

- Wash, peel, and cut all fruit into bite-sized pieces; substitute fruit that is in season at the time
- Pour orange juice on ripe banana pieces to prevent darkening
- Put all fruits and their juices in salad bowl and carefully mix together
- Serve in individual salad bowls, pour fruit sauce on fruit salad, and top with shredded coconut

Frozen Fruit Bites

2 cups chopped seasonal fresh fruit (pineapple, apples, grapes, strawberries, cantaloupe, etc.)
1 cup fruit sauce (see recipe on page 81) or crushed nuts (optional)

Directions

- Wash fruit and cut into bite-sized pieces
- Arrange on tray and put in freezer for 45–60 minutes
- Remove and serve as dessert
- Dip in fruit sauce or crushed nuts

Desserts

Fresh Fruit Popsicle

1 large mango
½ a pineapple
1 cup green grapes
1 tablespoon Sugar In The Raw® (optional)

Directions
- Wash all fruit
- Peel mango and pineapple, then dice
- Put all ingredients in blender and purée
- Pour into popsicle mold and freeze
- To remove popsicle, place popsicle mold in warm water for 1 minute to loosen
- Modify the recipe by using seasonal fresh fruit

Mango Coconut Pineapple Smoothie with Mint

1 cup diced mango
1 cup diced fresh pineapple
1 cup coconut milk
1 tablespoon Sugar In The Raw® (optional)

1 cup crushed ice
Mint leaves
Juice from the fruits

Directions
- Wash fruit and mint leaves
- Peel the mango, remove the seed, and dice
- Remove core from pineapple and dice
- Put all ingredients in blender, and purée well to make smoothie
- Garnish with mint leaf

Carolle's Homemade Banana Ice Cream

3–4 ripe bananas
1 cup almond milk (original or original vanilla)
½ cup coconut milk
½ tablespoon ground or grated nutmeg
½–1 tablespoon cinnamon powder
2 teaspoons ground vanilla beans
½ teaspoon sea salt (optional)
½ cup maple syrup or Sugar In The Raw®
2 tablespoons canola oil
1 tablespoon flaxseed meal

Directions

- Slice the bananas into small pieces and freeze
- Boil flaxseed meal in oil for 5 minutes on medium heat, stirring constantly
- Put frozen bananas and all other ingredients, except flaxseed meal/oil mixture, in blender and blend until smooth and thick, approximately 1–2 minutes
- Add flaxseed/oil mixture and continue blending for 1 minute more
- Return to freezer for 2 hours before serving
- May use other fresh fruit to make different flavors

Desserts

Homemade Coconut Ice Cream

2 cups almond milk (original)
4 cups coconut milk (freshly made)
1 tablespoon powdered vanilla beans
1 tablespoon grated nutmeg
1 tablespoon cinnamon powder
½ cup grated coconut for garnish
½ cup cherries for garnish (optional)

Directions

- Mix almond and coconut milk together in mixing bowl
- Add spices and whisk
- Put mixture in freezer for 1–2 hours until partially frozen
- Remove from freezer and whisk well until fluffy and expanded in amount
- Then pour in freezing container, cover and freeze
- Thaw a little before serving
- Garnish with shredded grated coconut before serving or serve with cake

Homemade Grape Nut/Vanilla Ice Cream

1 quart almond milk (original) or soy milk
1 tablespoon powdered vanilla beans
1 teaspoon ground or grated nutmeg
1 teaspoon cinnamon powder
¼ cup Sugar In The Raw®

1 cup Grape-Nuts cereal
2 tablespoons canola oil
2 tablespoons flaxseed meal
½ teaspoon sea salt (optional)

Directions

- Put milk in freezer and allow to half-freeze
- Cook flaxseed meal in oil for 5 minutes on medium heat
- Remove half-frozen milk from freezer
- Put all ingredients in blender except flaxseed meal and oil mixture
- Blend for 2 minutes, then add flaxseed/oil mixture and blend together for 1 minute more
- Pour into container and return to freeze for 2 hours prior to serving

Corn Hominy with Coconut and Almond Milk

2 cups dried corn hominy
4 cups water for soaking hominy
2 cups coconut milk
2 cups almond milk
2 teaspoons ground or grated nutmeg
1 tablespoon cinnamon powder

½ tablespoon ground vanilla beans
1 teaspoon sea salt
1 cup Sugar In The Raw® (for the whole pot)
4 cups water for cooking soaked hominy
Cinnamon sticks for garnish

Directions

- Rinse dry corn hominy in cold water and pick out any brown particles; then soak 2 cups hominy in 4 cups water for 1–2 hours, causing it to expand to approximately 4 cups hominy
- In large saucepan pour 4 cups water and 2 cups coconut milk and bring to a boil
- Add soaked hominy and cook on medium heat for 1–1 ½ hours
- Then add spices and almond milk and continue to cook for 30 minutes more or until tender and liquid is somewhat thickened
- Sweeten the entire amount or pour into cereal bowls and sweeten to taste and serve for breakfast or lunch

Beverages

Fresh Pineapple Delight

6 cups pineapple cubes or other seasonal fruit
6 fresh basil leaves
2 cups crushed ice

Directions

- Wash fruit and remove skin, if necessary
- Cut pineapple in chunks
- Put in blender with basil leaves and blend until smooth
- Serve with crushed ice or without

Fresh Fruit Shake

3–4 cups ripe fresh fruit (i.e. cantaloupe, pineapple, bananas, apple, strawberry)
½ cup lemon juice
1 cup crushed ice

Directions

- Wash and cut fruit in small pieces
- Put all of the fruit in a blender with any juice from the fruit; blend well
- Add crushed ice and continue blending for 1 minute

Jamaican-Style Sorrel Drink

2–3 cups fresh sorrel epicalyces (see glossary)
1 cup crushed fresh ginger
12 cups water
Sugar to taste (approximately 2–3 cups)
Sprigs of fresh peppermint
 or orange slices for garnish

Directions
- Bring 12 cups water to a boil in a large pot
- Wash ginger well and crush; add to boiling water and cook for 15–20 minutes
- Wash sorrel epicalyces well and put in boiling water with ginger; then cover pot
- Reduce heat to medium-low and allow sorrel to steep for 20–30 minutes
- Strain sorrel drink and sweeten to taste while warm
- Put in the refrigerator to chill
- Serve with crushed ice and a sprig of fresh peppermint and/or orange slices placed on the edge of the glass

Beverages

Fresh Hot Cerasee Beverage

6 fresh cerasee leaves
2–2 ½ cups water
Sugar In The Raw® to taste

Directions
- Wash leaves
- Pour 2–2 ½ cups water in saucepan and bring to a boil
- Add cerasee leaves to water
- Cover and continue to boil on medium heat for 10–15 minutes
- Strain into a cup and sweeten to taste

Hot Decaffeinated Lipton Tea

1 tea bag per cup of boiling water
Sugar In The Raw® (optional)

Directions

- Steep tea bag in boiling water (in cup or teapot) for 2 minutes
- Sweeten, if desired, with 1–2 teaspoons of sugar per cup
- May chill and use as iced tea by adding crushed ice

Hot Peppermint Beverage

6–8 fresh peppermint leaves per cup of water
2 cups water (or more)
Sugar In The Raw® (optional)

Directions

- Wash peppermint leaves and put in a pot of water
- Bring water to boil and boil for about 3–4 minutes
- Sweeten, if desired, with 1–2 teaspoons of Sugar In The Raw® per cup
- May chill and serve with crushed ice as a refreshing drink in summer

Fresh Squeezed Orange/Grapefruit Juice

Orange or grapefruit

Directions

- Wash orange and cut in halves
- Use juicer or squeeze juice from orange or grapefruit
- Remove seeds by straining
- Chill and serve (optional) or serve at room temperature

Miscellaneous

Homemade Cane Sugar

2 6-foot long sugar canes (or more if possible)
Sturdy grinder (metal if possible)
4–6 quart pot
Large cookie baking sheet (for hardening reduce cane liquid)

Directions

- Grow your own sugar cane or purchase some
- Wash sugar cane well
- Peel (optional) and cut up in pieces according to specific grinder
- Grind to extract juice, and then strain juice into saucepan
- Boil juice on medium to medium-high heat long enough to reduce it to a syrupy, thick consistency with visible granules
- Pour liquid on cookie sheet and allow to harden
- Once hardened cover with a towel and break into small pieces with a rolling pin or clean hammer
- Grind hardened chunks of sugar into sugar crystals
- Store in dry container for use

    1 gram of sugar = 4 calories
    1 teaspoon of sugar = 4 grams
    1 teaspoon of sugar = 16 calories

Sample Menu

Breakfast
1 glass water (room temperature)
½ to 1 cup fresh squeezed orange juice or 1 medium orange
½ to 1 cup cooked old-fashioned oatmeal with ½ cup almond milk and 2 tablespoons sugar (optional)
1 Soy Curl Fritter on 1–2 slices of whole wheat or gluten free toast or serve ½ cup tofu scramble on toast

Lunch/Dinner
1 glass water (room temperature)
1 cup multi-mix vegetable salad with dressing or sliced tomatoes and cucumbers
½ cup braised gluten strips with broccoli
½ to 1 cup Jamaican-Style Brown Rice and Red Beans
½ baked, steamed, or fried ripe plantain
1–2 scoops homemade mango ice cream

Supper
½ to 1 cup almond milk or ½ cup fruit juice or smoothie
1 peanut butter sandwich: 2 tablespoons peanut butter on 2 slices of bread (whole wheat or gluten free)

Weights and Measurements

Dry Measurements/Equivalents
3 teaspoons = 1 tablespoon = ½ oz. = 14.3 grams
2 tablespoons = 1/8 cup = 1 oz. = 28.3 grams
4 tablespoons = ¼ cup = 2 oz. = 56.7 grams
5 1/3 tablespoons = 1/3 cup = 2.6 oz. = 75.6 grams
8 tablespoons = ½ cup = 4 oz. = 113.4 grams
12 tablespoons = ¾ cup = 6 oz. = .375 pounds
32 tablespoons = 2 cups = 16 oz. = 1 pound

American Standard and Metric

Volume Dry
½ teaspoon = 2 ml
¾ teaspoon = 4 ml
1 teaspoon = 5 ml
1 tablespoon = 3 teaspoons = 15 ml
¼ cup = 50 ml
1/3 cup = 70 ml
½ cup = 118 ml
1 cup = 236 ml

Volume Liquid
2 tablespoon = 1 fl. oz. = 30 ml
¼ cup = 2 fl. oz. = 60 ml
½ cup = 4 fl. oz. = 125 ml
1 cup = 8 fl. oz. = 250 ml
2 cups = 1 pint = 16 fl. oz. = 500 ml
4 cups = 1 quart = 32 fl. oz. = 1000 ml or 1 liter
1 gallon = 4 quarts = 128 fl. oz. = 4 liters

Oven Temperatures
250 degrees Fahrenheit = 130 degrees Centigrade
300 degrees F = 150 degrees C
350 degrees F = 180 degrees C
375 degrees F = 190 degrees C
400 degrees F = 200 degrees C
425 degrees F = 220 degrees C
450 degrees F = 230 degrees C

Weight (Mass)
½ ounce = 15 grams
1 ounce = 30 grams
3 ounces = 85 grams
4 ounces = 115 grams
8 ounces = 225 grams
16 ounces = 450 grams

Resources and Reference Materials

Brandon, Leila. *A Merry Go Round of Recipes from Jamaica*. Kingston, Jamaica: Novelty Trading Co. Std..

Classic Middle Eastern Enticing Dishes from a Rich and Varied Cuisine. London, England: Anness Publishing Ltd., 2003.

Finley, Mark and Ernestine. *Lifestyle 2000: Secrets of Natural Living for the 21st Century.* Siloam Springs, AR: Creation Enterprises International, 1993.

Foster, Vernon. *New Start: New Health, New Energy, New Joy*. Weimer, CA: Weimer Institute, 1990.

Fowler, Sina Faye, Bessie Brooks West, and Grace Severance Shugart. *Food For 50.* 5th ed. New York, NY: John Wiley and Sons, Inc.

Fleetwood, Jennie and Filippelli, Marina. *The Illustrated Food and Cooking of The Caribbean Central and South America*. Blackfriars Rd. London. Anness Publishing Ltd., 2009

Friston, Kathy. *Veganist: Lose Weight, Get Healthy, Change The World*. New York, NY: Weinstein Books, 2011.

Gaylor, Paul. *Ultimate Vegetarian Cookbook*. New York, NY: D.K. Publishing Inc., 1999.

Goodhart, Robert S. and Maurice E. Shills. *Modern Nutrition in Health and Disease*. 5th ed. Philadelphia, PA: Lea and Febiger, 1975.

The Illustrated Kitchen Bible. 1st ed. New York, NY: Darling Kindersley Ltd., 2008.

Hildyard, Anne. *Appetizers 500: Best-Ever Recipes.* Blackfriars Road, London: Anness Publishing Ltd., 2009.

Holcomb, Carrie. *Easy Dinners Vegetarian*. Des Moines, IO: Meredith Books, 2005.

Joachim, David. *The Food Substitutions Bible.* Toronto, Ontario: Robert Rose Inc., 2005.

Levy, Marvin R., Mark Digman, and Janet H. Shirreffs. *Life and Health*. 5th ed. New York, NY: Random House, Inc., 1987.

Martin, Roberto. *Vegan Cooking for Carnivores*. New York, NY: Grand Central Publishing, 2012.

Orten, James M., and Otto W. Neuhause. *Human Biochemistry*. 9th ed. St. Louis, MO: C.V. Mosby Co., 1975.

Porth, Carol Matterson. *Pathophysiology*. Philadelphia, PA: Lippincott Co., 1986.

Rachor, JoAnn. *Of These Ye May Freely Eat: A Vegetarian Cookbook*. Sunfield, MI: Family Health Publications, 1990.

The Holy Bible, King James Version. Thomas Nelson Inc., 2003

Van Cleaves, Janice. *Food and Nutrition for Every Kid*. New York, NY: John Wiley and Sons, Inc., 1999.

Watt, Bernice K., and Annabel L. Merril. *Composition of Foods. Agricultural Handbook No. 8.* Washington, D.C., United States Department of Agriculture, 1963.

White, Ellen G. *Testimonies for the Church. Vol. 7.* Mountain View, CA: Pacific Press Publishing Association, 1948.

Glossary

Additives: Something added to foods for color.

Allergy: An immune response to a substance in foods, plants, drugs, or the environment. The focus here is on food or plant allergies. Some common allergic reactions are to gluten (or wheat and wheat products), soy and soy byproducts, nuts, fruits, lactose, etc.

Amino Acids: All living organisms contain protein. All proteins have as their building blocks substances called amino acids. Some amino acids are made by the cells of the organism and are called non-essential amino acids. Others must be supplied by food to the organism and are called essential since the organism cannot make them. These amino acids are isoleucine, fucine, lysine, methionine, cysteine, phenylalanine, tyrosine, threonine, tryptophan, and valine.

Artificial Sweetener: A sweetener that is not made from natural sources such as sugarcane, beets, and honey. An example of an artificial sweetener is aspartame.

Baking: A method of cooking in an oven using dry heat.

Berries: Fleshy fruits with seeds.

Carbohydrates: One of the important groups of macronutrients in the foods we eat, which is needed to provide energy to the body. Carbohydrates are chemically made of carbon, hydrogen, and oxygen (CH_2O). There are simple and complex carbohydrates. They are obtained mainly from plants. Each gram of CH_2O gives 4 calories.

Caffeine: A stimulant found in coffee, tea, chocolate (cocoa), and some soft drinks.

Celiac Disease: A condition developed in childhood by the malabsorption of fats and indigestion of starch due to intolerance to gluten and other wheat byproducts.

Cerasee (Momordica charantia): A vine bearing a small bumpy skinned yellow or orange fruit. The leaves are used to make a bitter herbal tea that is regarded for its medicinal and purgative properties.

Cooking Directions: Ways of cooking foods, such as baking, boiling, braising, broiling, frying, sautéing, and steaming.

Dietary Guidelines for Americans: A set of recommendations by the USDA and DHHS encouraging a diet that includes a variety of foods to provide adequate intake of protein, carbohydrates, fats, vitamins, minerals, and fiber.

Enzymes: Protein substances in the cells of the body that control or speed up chemical reactions without themselves being changed

Essential Amino Acids (see Amino Acids): Are those that the body cannot make in sufficient amounts to supply all the needs of the body, so they must be a part of the daily diet.

Essential Nutrients: Important nutrients that cannot be made in the body (or in inadequate amounts) and must be supplied by diet.

Fats: This is one of the basic four macronutrients needed by the body. Fats are of animal and plant (vegetable) origin. They are the most concentrated form of energy and supply 9 calories for every 1 gram of fat. Fats consist of triglycerides made up of fatty acids and glycerol. Fatty acids consist of carbon, hydrogen, and oxygen (CHO). Animal fat is saturated and contains cholesterol. Vegetable/plant fats contain no cholesterol and are referred to as unsaturated.

Fertilizers: Chemicals put in the soil to enrich it, which are often artificial. A natural fertilizer that works well is manure.

FDA: The Food and Drug Administration is an agency of the U.S. Department of Agriculture, which functions to ensure that the foods we buy and eat are safe.

Fiber: Is a non-nutritive substance that is necessary in one's diet. It is also referred to as roughage or bulk. It consists of indigestible carbohydrates, such as the cellulose in fruits, vegetables, nuts, grains, e.g. the skin and the bran of wheat. Fiber is a necessary substance in the digestive process, helping to bind other waste products to water for excretion and preventing constipation.

First Diet: God gave man the first diet as we read in Genesis 1:29, which says "Behold, I have given you every herb bearing seed, which is upon the face of all the earth, and every tree, in the which is the fruit of a tree yielding seed; to you it shall be for meat."

Food: Substances taken into the body of living things (plants or animals) to promote the growth and repair of tissue, provide energy, and enhance other life processes. Food is usually of animal or plant origin.

Food Labeling: This is the way to find out the nutrients and ingredients that are in packaged and processed foods or even in packaged ingredients that you buy. Read labels on the packages, bottles, or cans and look at what item is first on the list of ingredients. They are written in order of greatest amount to the least amount in the product. Labeling tells the serving size and number of servings in the container and the percentage of the Recommended Dietary Allowances for Americans (USRDA). Read all labels.

Fruit: The part of the plant that contains the seeds.

Glucose: Is a simple sugar (or monosaccharide) that forms a half of most other forms of sugar (such as sucrose, lactose, galactose). It is also sometimes called "blood sugar." Glucose is an efficient fuel used by the brain and nervous system. When it is metabolized in the presence of oxygen, it produces carbon dioxide and water.

Gluten: Protein found in wheat flour and used much in entrée dishes of vegans and vegetarians. It is elastic in nature and insoluble in water. There is gluten flour, which is ready for use in making vegan/vegetarian "meats." When water is added to it, then you see the elasticity.

Gluten Free: Many people have allergic reactions to gluten and all wheat products, so it is important to read labels to ensure there is no wheat product in the foods and ingredients they buy. Children and adults with celiac disease are intolerant to gluten. These people need a gluten free diet, so rice or corn flour may be used as substitutes.

Glossary

GMO: Genetically Modified Organisms have been used for more than 25 years. These are plants and animals created through "gene splicing" by genetic engineering. This process merges DNA of different species of plants and animals to create new but unstable combinations of plants and animals, bacterial and viral genes that could not occur naturally by crossbreeding. GMOs are not considered safe, but they are in conventional and some organic foods. Because there is no mandatory USDA labeling, the "Non-GMO Project Verified seal" was created by an organization of retailers to give consumers in North America access to clearly labeled Non-GMO foods and information they deserve. To learn more, visit the Non-GMO Project website (http://1ref.us/7i).

Honey: Sweet substance made by bees and used in place of sugar. It has the same caloric level as sugar. True vegans do not use honey because it is an animal product.

Hormones: Secretions by ductless (endocrine) glands of the body that flow directly into the bloodstream or lymph nodes. They affect the functioning of organs and act as stimulant accelerators. Examples are insulin by the pancreas, thyroxine by the thyroid gland, adrenalin by the adrenal gland, and testosterone by the testes.

Humus: Dark soil made up of decayed leaves. This is a natural fertilizer.

Immune: Protection against something harmful, like a disease.

Immune System: System (of the body and outside) that protects the body from disease by producing antibodies.

Iodine: Non-metallic element obtained mostly from seaweed. It is needed by the body in trace amounts. It is used as a treatment of thyroid disease. It is also used as a test for starch, which is a compound. A compound with starch turns blue when tested with iodine.

Iodized Salt: Table salt treated with iodine, a source of dietary iodine.

Iron: Common metallic element found in some foods, water, and certain minerals. It is present in the body in small amounts, but is mostly found in red blood cells. It is important in the body processes transferring oxygen to the tissues and the brain. Some iron is stored in the liver, spleen, bone marrow, and some is excreted in feces. Iron must be daily supplied by diet. Iron deficiency can lead to anemia, at which point supplements may need to be taken.

Juice: Liquid from fruits, vegetables, or cooked meats.

Juicing: The process of retrieving juice from fruits or vegetables using a juicer.

Lactose: Sugar in milk.

Lactose Intolerant: Inability to digest milk sugar, lactose.

Lacto-ovo: A vegetarian who uses milk and eggs.

Liquid Aminos: A vegetable protein seasoning made from healthy non-GMO Project Certified soybeans that is alcohol free, gluten-free, unfermented, without preservatives and contains 16 amino acids. It is used in place of salt (in small amounts). Look for Bragg Liquid Aminos with the "Non-GMO Project Verified Seal."

Malnutrition: Poor nutrition due to a diet lacking in some essential nutrients or having an excess of one.

Macronutrients: Nutrients needed by the body in certain amounts as suggested by the RDA. These are protein, carbohydrates, fats, and also water.

Micronutrients: Nutrients needed by the body in small amounts to help in the chemical processes such as growth and metabolism as carried out in the body.

Naseberry (Sapodilla): The fruit of the sapodilla; a tropical fruit with a rough brownish skin and very sweet brownish pulp.

Natural Foods: Foods grown without artificial fertilizers, sometimes called organic.

Non-GMO: Not having genetically modified organisms; to be GMO-free.

Non-GMO Project Verified: A nonprofit organization set up by a group of retailers to offer consumers "independent verification of testing and GMO controls for products in the U.S. and Canada." Their seal of verification assures that a product is produced without GMO or with very low risk of contamination.

Nutmeg: An aromatic seed that is used as a spice and is produced by a tree of the genus Myristica.

Nutrients: The nutritious substances in food that help in growth and other body processes to provide energy and keep the body healthy.

Nutrition: The science that deals with the process by which living organisms take in and assimilate food for growth, energy, and repair of worn out tissues.

Nutritional Yeast Flakes: A deactivated yeast that is sold commercially as a food product in the form of flakes.

Organic: Chemical substance that contains carbon; relating to the process of growing or producing goods naturally without artificial fertilizers.

Organic Foods: Foods grown with natural fertilizer such as humus.

Pattie: Vegan or vegetarian, rounded or oblong shaped (like a hamburger). Made from veggie meats, legumes, nuts; baked or fried; served on a bun/roll.

Patty: A delicious crescent-shaped turnover. Filling can be seasoned meat and vegetables, legumes, or veggie meat in a dainty crust. It can be used as an appetizer or hors d'oeuvres or served for lunch or dinner.

Preservatives: Substances, e.g. sugar, salt, or chemicals, used to prevent food spoilage. Vegans do not use foods preserved with chemicals.

Protein: One of the macronutrients needed by the body for growth and repair of worn out tissues. It is one of the essential nutrients.

RDA: Recommended Daily Allowances is the average daily level of intake of any nutrient sufficient to meet the needs of nearly all healthy people. These are established guidelines by the Food and Nutrition Board of the National Research Council branch of the Academy of Sciences.

Glossary

Sorrel: A member of the hibiscus, okra, and cotton family; grows erect and is sparsely branched. Sorrel is an acid and has edible leaves and flowers and a familiar flavor similar to the cranberry.

Soy: Product of a soybean.

Soybean: Originated in southeast Asia and used in China about 1100 BC. By the first century AD, soybeans were grown in Japan and many other countries. In the 1870s, soybeans increased in popularity and were first grown in the United States to feed to livestock. It was in 1904 that George Washington Carver discovered that soybeans are a valuable source of protein and oil. He also realized the benefits of soybeans for preserving good quality soil. He encouraged the rotation of crops by the cotton farmers. Soybeans were wholesome, but they have been somewhat contaminated in recent years since the birth of GMOs.

Soy Isolate: Dehydrated byproduct of soybeans. Used in making many vegan or vegetarian meat substitutes.

Starch: A digestible complex carbohydrate found in foods from plants such as cereals, breads, potatoes, grains, legumes, etc.

Sugar: A simple carbohydrate (called a saccharide); sweet carbohydrate found in sugarcane, beets, agave, honey, etc. It is better to use these natural sugars rather than artificial sweeteners.

Sugar Cane: Tall tropical grass grown for its sugar.

Tofu: Bean curd and soybean curd; made from cooked soybean. It is bland, so it will absorb any flavor and seasoning in which it is marinated. It comes in textures such as silk, soft, firm, and extra firm. It is available in health food stores and supermarkets. Look for the seals "Non-GMO Project Verified" and "USDA Organic."

TVP: Textured Vegetable Protein is made from soybeans. Usually dehydrated so it must be rehydrated before use. Look for the "Non-GMO Project Verified" and "USDA Organic" seals.

USDA: United States Department of Agriculture.

USDA Organic Seal: Seal signifying that farmers use methods that preserve the environment and avoid using pesticides and antibiotics to grow crops or raise animals.

Vanilla Bean: Used to make dark aromatic vanilla flavoring. There are three types that are most common: 1) Bourbon Madagascar vanilla bean, 2) the thicker Mexican bean, and the 3) Tahitian vanilla bean. Vanilla beans are available whole or in powder form.

Vanilla Extract: Made from the vanilla bean by soaking it in alcohol. The imitation extract has a similar flavor, but is often made from wood pulp byproducts from the paper industry. It is safer to use vanilla bean powder than vanilla extract.

Vegan: A vegetarian who uses no animal products—meat, milk, eggs, or honey. Some vegans do not purchase clothing or furniture that is made from animal products. A vegan uses organic or naturally grown foods.

Veganism: The practice of eating and sometimes using no animal product; using naturally grown fruits, vegetables, nuts, and seeds.

Vegetables: The part of the plant that does not contain the seed—the leaf, root, and stem.

Vegetarian: One who eats no animal meat, but sometimes uses dairy and egg. Another name for this type of person is lacto-ovo vegetarian.

Vegetarianism: The practice of eating a diet of fruits, nuts, vegetables, and seeds that usually includes some dairy, eggs, and honey.

Vitamins: One of the micronutrients needed by the body to use other nutrients to help in growth metabolism. They are found in foods and are supplied in a well-balanced diet. They are needed in small amounts.

Water: Very important macronutrient required for all body functions. Water constitutes approximately 70 percent of our body weight. Ideal daily intake is approximately 50 percent of one's body weight in ounces.

Index

A
Ackee, 41
    Lemon Coconut Sauce, 83
Almond Meal, 29
Almond Milk, 24
Appetizers, 23-30
Apple Raisin Millet Cake, 89
Arroz con Curles de Soyas (Rice and Soy Curls), 39

B
Banana Fritters, 24
Banana Ice Cream, 96
Bar-B-Q Sauce, Homemade, 80
Basic Nutrition, 17
Beans and Rice, 60-61
Beans and Vegetable Combo, 70
Bean Soup, 71
Beverages, Cold and Hot, 99-102
Biscuits, Nadia's Homemade, 87
Braised Gluten Roast Strips, 34
Brazil Nut Sauce, 80
Bread, Ezekiel, 87
Breadfruit, Steamed, 67
Bread Pudding, 93
Brown Gravy, 79
Brown Rice, 47, 49, 61
Brussel Sprouts, Oven Roasted, 74
Bulgur Wheat, Seasoned, 61

C
Cabbage with Soy Curls, 41
Cake, Vegan Dump, 89
Cane, Sugar, 103
Candied Sweet Potatoes (Yam), 64
Carolle's Cream of Pumpkin Soup, 23, 69
Carolle's Fresh Tropical Fruit Salad, 94
Carolle's Pasta Salad, 66
Carolle's Veggie Patties, 57-58
Carrot and Beet Sauce, 84
Cashew Cheese, 85
Cashew Cheese Sauce, 80
Cashew Cheese Spread, Dip, 83
Cauliflower Steak with Curry Sauce, 75
Cerasee (Momordica charanta), 107
Cerassee Beverage- Fresh Hot, 101
Chickpeas (Garbanzo) Rounds, 45
Coconut, 91, 94
Coconut Ice Cream, 97
Coconut Milk, Cream, 23, 42, 61, 62, 69, 71, 80, 81, 88, 89, 91-98
Coconut Sauce, 42, 46, 81, 83, 91
Collard Greens with Soy Chips, 74
Corn Hominy, 98
Cornmeal pudding, 91
Creamy Mac 'N Cashew Cheese, 62
Curried Gluten Bits, 36
Curried Mushrooms and Soy Chips (or TVP), 40
Curried Seasoned Soy Curls, Plain, 38
Curried Tofu/Gluten Mince Scramble, 44
Curry Powder, 36, 38, 40, 41, 44, 47, 49, 57, 59, 75
Curry Sauce, 75

D
Desserts, 89-98
Gluten Free, 108
Dressings, 77-78
Dr. U's Potato Salad, 64
Dump Cake, 89

Healthful Living Cookbook

E
Eggplant, 76
Egg Substitute, 20
Entrées, 33-59
Ezekiel Bread, 87

F
Flour, unbleached, 57, 92
    Gluten, 28, 33-38, 44, 46, 48, 52, 56, 57, 93, 108
    Gluten-Free, 108
    Rice, 23, 24, 27, 55, 79, 80, 88
    Whole Wheat, 23, 24, 27-29, 33, 35, 45, 54-59, 62, 87-90, 93, 94
Fresh Fruit Shake, 99
Fresh Pineapple Delight, 99
Fresh Fruit Popsicle, 95
Fresh Tropical Fruit Salad, 94
Fritters
    Banana, 24
    Soy Curls, 27
    Vere's Pumpkin, 29
Frozen Fruit Bites, 94
Fruit and Nut Bread Pudding, 93

G
Gluten, 108
Gluten Chick Patties, 35
Gluten Chick Salad, Hot or Cold, 37
Gluten Free Flour, 108
Gluten Free Sauces, 80, 81, 83-85
Gluten Mince, 34
GMO, 16, 20, 109, 110, 111
Gluten Roast, 33, 34
Green Beans, Whole, and Potato Salad, 65
Green Banana's, boiled (with Ackee and Soy Curls), 41

H
Homemade Block Cheese, 85
Hors d' oeuvres, Meatballs, 28
Hummus, Spicy Homemade, 82
Hungry Man Veggie Wrap, 46

I

J
Jamaican-Style Rice and Red Beans, 60, 61
Jamaican-Style Sorrel Drink, 100, 111

K

L
Lemon Ackee Coconut Sauce, 83
Lemon Garlic Dressing, 78
Lima Beans and Mushrooms, Sautéed, Curried, 49

M
Macaroni 'N Cheese, Creamy, 62
Mango Coconut, Pineapple Smoothie, 95
Meatballs, Hors d' oeuvres, 28
Meatballs, Vegan/Vegetarian, 53
Meatloaf, Vegan, 52
Mix Beans and Vegetable Combo, 70
Multimix Vegetable Salad, 73

N

Naseberry (Sapodilla), 110
Non-GMO, 16, 20, 109, 110
Nut Curry, 47
Nutrition Information, 17
Nut Loaf, 48
Nutmeg, 110
Nuts, Nuts, Nuts, 25
Nut Roast, Vegan, 51
Nutritional Yeast Flakes, 110

O

Organic, 15, 20, 110
Organic Foods, 110
Oven Roasted Brussel Sprouts, 74

P

Parsley/Cilantro Sauce, 85
Pasta Salad, Carolle's, 66
Patties
    Carolle's Veggie, 57-58
    Gluten Chick, 35
    Split Peas/Nut, 50
    Veggie Subway, 59
Peanut Butter/Almond Sauce, 84
Peas
    Chick, 45
    Pigeon, 61
    Red, 60-61
Pineapple Delight, Fresh, 99
Plantain, Baked Ripe Sweet, 66
Potatoes, Candied, Sweet with
    Orange Sauce, 64
Potato Salad, Dr. U's, 64
Potato and Green Bean Salad, Nadia's, 65
Pudding
    Cornmeal, 91
    Fruit, Nut Bread, 93
    Sweet Potato, 92

Pumpkin Bites, 26
Pumpkin Fritters, Vere's, 29
Pumpkin Soup, Carolle's Cream of, 23, 69

Q

R

Red or Pink Beans Soup, 71
Rice and Red Beans, Jamaican-Style, 60-61
Roast
    Gluten, 33
    Vegan Nut, 51
Rounds, Chick Peas (Garbanzo), 45

S

Salad
    Carolle's Pasta, 66
    Dr. U's Potato, 64
    Fresh Tropical Fruit, 94
    Gluten Chick (Hot or Cold), 37
    Multimix Vegetable, 73
    Nadia's Potato and String Beans, 65
    Tabbouleh on Lettuce, 73
Salsa, Homemade, 30
Sautéed Curried Lima Beans
    and Mushrooms, 49
Seasoned Bulgur Wheat, 61
Seasoned Collard Greens, 74
Side Dishes, 60-67
Soy Chips (or TVP) with Mushrooms, 40
Soy Curls
    and Ackee, 41
    Fritters, 27
    Plain Curried Seasoned, 38
Sorrel, 111
Sorrel Drink, Jamaican-Style, 100
Split Peas and Nut Patties, 50

Steamed Breadfruit with Basil, 67
Stir Fry Vegetables with Gluten Roast Strips, 38
Sweet Potato Pie, Carolle's, 90
Sweet Potato Pudding, 92
Sweet Potato (Yam) Wedges, Baked, 63

T
Tabbouleh Salad on Romaine Lettuce, 73
Tea, Lipton Decaffeinated, 102
Tofu/Gluten Mince Scramble, Curried, 44
Tofu Logs, Bar-B-Q Sauce, 43
Tofu Logs in Coconut Sauce, 42
Tomato Basil Dressing, Homemade, 77

U

V
Vanilla, 111
Vanilla Beans, 111
Vanilla Extract, 111
Vanilla, Imitation, Alcohol Free, 111
Vegan, 15-17, 111
Vegan Mayonnaise, 78
Vegekabob, 56
Vegetable Carrousel and Dip, 28
Vegetable Salad, Multimex, 73
Vegetarian, 15, 112
Veggie Patties, Carolle's, 57-58
Veggie Soup Base Seasoning, 77
Veggie Subway Pattie, 59

W
Water, 20, 112
Wheat, Bulgur, Seasoned, 61

X

Y
Yam, 64
Candied Sweet Potatoes, 64
Sweet Potato Wedges, 63

About the Author

Carolle Walker has been a health and nutrition-driven person since she was seven years old. She watched her grandma cook (and she was very good), began trying to imitate her, and hoped that she would grow up to be a good cook who could help others to eat healthy. She continued to gain interest in cooking, which quickly became a hobby. While in high school she tried creating a few dishes using fresh fruits, vegetables, and foods from her father's garden or the market. She heard about vegetarianism but had very little knowledge about it.

Later she attended West Indies College in Jamaica, West Indies (now called Northern Caribbean University), where the meals were all lacto-ovo vegetarian. This is where she gained a lot of knowledge about vegetarianism. She graduated with a certificate and diploma in elementary education with a concentration in home economics. Thus began her serious journey toward a vegetarian lifestyle.

Upon graduating she accepted a position teaching home economics at a technical high school in Kingston, Jamaica. In her free time she continued experimenting with new vegetarian dishes, which she shared with her housemates. In 1971 she relocated to New York to study nutrition, completing a certificate in quantity cookery and dietetics from the New York Institute of Dietetics. It was then that she became aware of many things that the U.S. Department of Agriculture allows in our foods and in the food industry, which caused her to choose to avoid eating animal products and discouraged her from eating away from home.

Her increased interest in nutrition and vegetarianism led her to Pratt Institute in Brooklyn, New York, where she researched vegetarianism and received a bachelor's degree in food science and management in 1975. She worked as a dietitian in various nursing homes and a health-related facility before pursuing and completing a master's degree in nutrition education from New York University in 1980. While studying for her master's degree, she focused a lot on human biochemistry with special emphasis on vitamins and minerals along with the other macronutrients. She was also a member of the American Dietetic Association (now the Academy of Nutrition and Dietetics) while at NYU and several years following graduation.

During her career she worked as a dietitian in a research program for clients with eating disorders at New York State Psychiatric Hospital, then as director of a nutrition program at a health center in Brooklyn, New York. Later she worked as a nutritionist and nutrition educator with nutrition groups and health departments from New York to Florida.

On her journey toward veganism, Carolle's main guide was the Bible, and specifically Genesis 1:29. Here God, the Creator of the universe and humanity, gave Adam the first and best diet of fruits, nuts, seeds, and vegetables—a "vegan" diet. Throughout the years Carolle continued to engage in her hobbies of creating recipes, cooking, hosting dinners, and gardening. All the while she shared with many the nutritious, delicious vegan/vegetarian meals she created. Her experiences with food, nutrition, and diet therapy have resulted in recipes that are tasty, nutritionally adequate, and well balanced according to Dietary Guidelines for Americans. Over the years she has conducted vegan and vegetarian cooking and nutrition education classes at her church in an effort to encourage "behavior modification" related to veganism/vegetarianism.

The *Healthful Living Cookbook: Caribbean Style* began in the 1990s when Carolle was a lacto-ovo vegetarian. Now as a vegan, she has rewritten this book to highlight vegan cooking.

We invite you to view the complete
selection of titles we publish at:

www.TEACHServices.com

Scan with your mobile
device to go directly
to our website.

Please write or email us your praises, reactions, or thoughts
about this or any other book we publish at:

info@TEACHServices.com

TEACH Services, Inc., titles may be purchased in bulk for
educational, business, fund-raising, or sales promotional use.
For information, please e-mail:

BulkSales@TEACHServices.com

Finally, if you are interested in seeing
your own book in print, please contact us at

publishing@TEACHServices.com

We would be happy to review your manuscript for free.

www.ingramcontent.com/pod-product-compliance
Lightning Source LLC
Chambersburg PA
CBHW080551170426
43195CB00016B/2752